From the

Game Warden's Campfire

True Stories from a Retired Kentucky Game Warden

JEFF FINN

FROM THE GAME WARDEN'S CAMPFIRE

Message from the Author

Thank you to those who enjoyed my first book, *"From the Game Warden's Desk,"* and gave me a kind word. I hope you enjoy this second one also.

I realize I'm not a polished writer. I strive to be a simple storyteller of a few true-life adventures. Please pull up a chair to my campfire and relax as I share a few more true game warden tales.

Jeff Finn
retired KY game warden

TABLE OF CONTENTS

FROM THE GAME WARDEN'S CAMPFIRE

FROM THE GAME WARDEN'S CAMPFIRE

The Raw Fur Task Force

Being the game warden always brought new challenges and experiences. On one occasion, I received a report that someone had a large amount of illegal raw fur. State law regulated how and when you could possess unprocessed pelts. This tip, however, came from something other than my familiar sources. The informant stated that the raw fur was inside a freezer located in a home.

Usually, when it came to being informed of illegal possessions inside a freezer, it often came from former girlfriends or ex-wives. Some angry women would gladly give written statements to the game warden if it got the man in trouble who did them wrong. However, my source this time was not a mad woman. It was the leader of the regional drug task force who gave me this information.

While executing a search warrant during a previous drug raid, task force officers found many raw raccoon pelts in a freezer. It occurred during the closed season when possession was illegal. I told the task force leader I would need a statement to secure a search warrant for the pelts. He said a written report was not a problem but advised me that a possible drug lab was back in operation in that home. I got my search warrant for the wildlife violations, and we joined forces in case I would be entering an active drug lab to seize these pelts.

I had served plenty of search warrants by then, but this was the first time I had done one quite like this. The drug task force team would handle the initial takedown, and then the task force leader and I would conduct our search. Usually, it would have taken a lot more planning for security reasons on my part. I asked their leader what I needed to do. He looked at me, smiled, shrugged, and said, "Nothing, this is what these guys live for."

So, on the night of our operation, I met him and his team at the Jefferson Davis Monument State Park in Fairview, Kentucky. I chatted with the leader while watching a group of burly men getting equipped with helmets and riot gear. There were no doubts they knew what they were doing and had done this often.

We all loaded up to head over to the house. Their leader told me he and I simply needed to stay out of their way until they gave us the "all clear" signal. We reached the house, and I watched as a line of task force soldiers trotted to the door while surrounding the house.

I heard a booming knock and the words "search warrant." After that, things got intense.

The whole thing was loud and happened fast. A minute later, we received the "all clear" signal. It was time for the task force leader and me to enter the home.

You hear stories of doors getting kicked or blown off their hinges. That did not happen here. The outside door was still firmly connected to its hinges and the door frame.

The door frame, however, was flat on the ground, with the door still very much attached to it. The task force team had hit this door so hard that the only thing left was a hole in the wall. The leader and I walked through that giant gaping hole in the side of the house to find everything and everybody under complete control.

Someone had been killing many raccoons. I found over seventy fur pelts in the freezer. In court, I prosecuted the wildlife charges and gained a new respect for those officers working in our drug task forces.

Don't do drugs. You do not want those guys coming through a hole in the wall where you used to have a door.

FROM THE GAME WARDEN'S CAMPFIRE

The Red Light District

Poachers in boats on large rivers know one thing. They realize the boat ramp is the most likely spot to be checked by the game warden. In my previous book, I told a story of outlaws who took steps to avoid bringing out their illegal haul at the ramp. They knew it was a likely place to get caught. This next story is similar. These guys took extra precautions.

I worked with my fellow game wardens on a district patrol one night. All the men in our area were working together, along with two officers flying in an airplane. Our eyes in the sky were looking for illegal activity so they could direct the closest ground officers to catch the poachers.

It was late into the night. Our men saw a flash of light while flying over the Green River. The "Green" was one of the larger rivers in our district, and this light was different.

Most spotlights and flashlights we observed were white. Occasionally, like this time, we came across a red light. Red lights usually meant we were looking at fur poachers. Their glow does not frighten wildlife the way bright lights do.

The game wardens in the plane said there was a boat on Green River with fur poachers in it. They watched the active red light as it shined on the banks, looking for fur-bearing wildlife. When poaching from boats, raccoons were usually the big haul in cases like this, although mink, fox, muskrat, and other animals would not get passed up.

There was little doubt that we were observing illegal poaching. At one point, one of our observers said. "Oh, he loves his red light! He is shining it everywhere!" Any slight doubt about their legality soon turned into zero doubt when the officers in the plane started seeing muzzle flashes from shots fired by the boat's occupants.

The radio talk started cranking up. Plans came together to get whichever game wardens were the closest to the boat ramp to wait for these outlaws. I was driving one truck with a man riding with me. There were two other officers in another vehicle. They were closer. My partner and I would be serving as backup.

The closest officers reached the boat ramp. They started getting set up and then got hidden. Soon, we should be catching poachers. Everything was looking good until it wasn't.

The game wardens in the airplane now told the ones near the ramp to "Go! Go! Go!" They said to jump in your trucks fast and get out of there!

Our illegal fur takers were making a pitstop. On their way to the boat ramp, they stopped underneath the Green River Parkway bridge. Now, the officers in the plane observed our poachers while they packed items from the boat to the bridge. Their craft was getting much lighter while they stashed carcasses near the parkway above.

Even without seeing the dead animals from the plane, game wardens instinctively know what is happening while watching flashlights go up and down a riverbank multiple times in a case like this.

These poachers would not be approaching the boat ramp with any apparent violations. Thankfully, tonight, the airplane would allow us to monitor what occurred after these poachers took off the river and left the boat ramp.

Our two game warden trucks had to hide at different locations now. The eyes in the sky would watch the poachers while they drove from the boat ramp to the parkway bridge.

As expected, a truck hauling a boat soon pulled over and stopped beside the southbound bridge on the parkway. A far-off airplane with two game wardens watched as flashlights made multiple trips under the bridge.

These guys had this down to a science; however, outboard engine noise and later parkway traffic motors had drowned out the sound of a high-flying airplane drifting across the night sky in blackout mode with no lights. That will throw a kink into your science.

After reloading the boat with the many animal carcasses stashed under the bridge, our crew took off down the parkway. The two game wardens in the nearest vehicle now hustled to catch up to them. My partner and I were even further behind. I had to do some fast driving to make up the difference.

The first game wardens could now see the poachers in front of them on the parkway. Before they put the blue lights on, they radioed me. They did not want this turning into a high-speed chase down this four-lane highway. "Put your gas pedal to the floor and get in front of these outlaws," they said. They wanted my truck to block them if they decided to run when the blue lights came on. We had already seen them going to great lengths to avoid getting caught, and we didn't want to see any more of that.

Now I'm flying down the dark parkway. I finally see two sets of headlights in front of me. As soon as I pass a department truck, I'm coming up beside a pickup, hauling a boat. My partner and I look at them as their heads snap to the left to see game wardens coming around. For a quick flash in time, all our eyes meet. We liked that flash a lot more than they did. If I could ever get Norman Rockwell to paint me a picture, it would be of that one second in time.

The second I pass, blue lights turn on behind them. They quickly realize they are squeezed between two law enforcement vehicles and pull over to the side.

Exiting our vehicles, we find a boat full of dead raccoons. Arrests and seizures followed. It made me wonder how many times they had gotten away with this. On this night, it was going to cost them dearly.

The Early Days

Simpson County, Kentucky, was my first county assignment as a state game warden. It was also the county where I grew up. After becoming the wildlife officer, I immediately heard complaints about one individual. The callers all claimed he poached many deer.

Growing up there, I already knew this man. Even though I heard his name often, I rarely ran into him. He was no dummy. He usually stayed hidden while he was out hunting. I listened to so many complaints across the county. If there had been a poster for the most wanted wildlife violator, his picture would have been on it.

I often worked in areas looking for illegal spotlighting of deer. Despite all the complaints, I never checked this guy on my patrols. That all changed one day following a phone call.

Someone had finally had enough, and this informant was mad. The caller had some excellent information. They told me where to find a nice whitetail buck carcass hanging in a barn. This deer had a bullet hole; it was not the firearm season.

The farmer who owned the land permitted me to look inside his barn. I took another game warden along with me. We entered the barn and saw a nice buck hanging from the rafters. The deer was not correctly tagged, which made it illegal no matter what type of weapon killed it.

The poacher now saw game wardens visiting this barn. He no longer stayed hidden as he came to join us. This guy was mad and running his mouth a lot. He claimed this was all a simple mistake. He started waving around a Tennessee deer tag. He claimed the buck was legal, saying it was a Tennessee deer. He was cagey and had planned for a situation like this in advance.

His story, like his buck, was full of holes. The tag had not been on the deer as it should have been. The deer was not legally validated (checked in) before leaving Tennessee. We told him the deer was going with us, and he was getting a citation. As suspected, he did not take that well.

Now, his mouth went into overdrive. He ran over to the other older game warden, telling him he was not welcome on this property. That game warden looked at him and said, "If you don't calm down and quit acting like a fool, I know some property downtown you'll be sleeping on tonight."

Being irate and realizing it was over, he walked by me and whispered. "I'm going to have to burn you now."

I wanted the other officer to be a witness to that statement, so I told him to repeat what he said. He stared at me and would not repeat it. Before this day, I had heard reports of barns burned by this man. Some said he was very vindictive.

We ended up taking the dead deer and citing him. We also seized the Tennessee deer tag. I did take precautions following his threat.

I had a wife, a baby, and a toddler. If he had come to my house to "burn" me that night, it would not have ended well for him. Depending on which end of the place he showed up, my brother and I were waiting with shotguns.

Since we knew he planned to argue in court that the deer came from Tennessee, we filed federal charges against him for bringing illegal wildlife across state lines. I knew this poached animal died in Simpson County, Kentucky. I knew the exact farm. However, I did not want to make good people testify who hoped to protect their barns from getting burned.

Stubbornness and pride can cost you more than honesty. The poacher could have admitted what happened and saved money. His "Tennessee" lie cost him way more in federal court than the truth would have cost in state court.

FROM THE GAME WARDEN'S CAMPFIRE

We All Remember the Day

It was a Thursday, March 19th, 1987, and I was at home. I received a call from my friend and working partner, game warden Tom Culton. Tom wasted no time before saying, "Bob Banker has been shot and killed." Those words hit me hard.

Officer Bob Banker was the game warden in Christian County, Kentucky, while I served in Logan County. There was one county in between us. A few weeks earlier, all three of us officers from those counties had worked together on one day. I had no idea it would be the last time I saw Bob alive.

On the day of Officer Banker's murder, I had been a game warden for four years. During those four years, I often received questions from someone asking how they could become a conservation officer. Following that one day, those questions seemed to stop for several years. That event brought home the dangers of the job.

Officer Banker was out doing his job on March 19th. He had checked a person's fishing license and then issued him a ticket for fishing without one. He was walking away from the violator when this individual shot him in the back and killed him over a minor citation.

A farmer nearby yelled for the murderer to stop shooting the officer. The gunman turned on the farmer and shot him, wounding him. The killer stole the deceased officer's citation booklet to hide his identity but later got caught. The ticket book was in the trunk of his car when he was apprehended.

We grieved for the loss of our law enforcement brother. Officer Banker left behind his wife and two small children.

For months following this incident, many routine checks on sportsmen just seemed different. Game wardens were taking even more safety precautions. Several of those we checked were nervous and on edge.

One officer started to do a routine check on a man fishing. This person had a pistol with him. It was legal for him to have the gun. The fisherman saw the officer's truck but did not see the game warden. He feared having this pistol with him since he knew about Officer Banker's murder. The man fishing decided to hide his legal gun.

The game warden watched all this. The officer, asking himself why this man was hiding a gun, went on the alert. Nothing illegal happened here, but the senseless murder had caused many to overthink everything they usually did.

One day during this period, I was checking fishing on the Red River at the Dot community in my county. I parked my marked patrol vehicle near the bridge and left on foot. I eased up the riverbank heading upstream. I saw a Jon boat running down the river in my direction.

When the man in the boat saw my patrol truck, he immediately grabbed a gun. I was hiding while watching this. Soon, he started throwing handfuls of items out into the river. I often watched people throwing fish back when they had caught too many. They did the same for undersized ones. I wasn't sure what this man was throwing, but it wasn't fish.

When he got close enough where I could check him, a nervous man asked me if it was okay to have a gun in the boat if he had no bullets. It was then I realized what I had seen hitting the water earlier. I had watched him take handfuls of 22 rifle cartridges and toss them in the river. Once again, the game warden's murder had caused an honest man to doubt himself.

I told him it was legal for him to have his gun and his bullets. Many folks I checked fishing were afraid of snakes and kept a small snake gun with them. Then I saw a single shiny 22 cartridge he had missed in the bottom of his Jon boat. I said, "Look there, you do have a bullet." The still nervous man picked it up quickly and tossed it in the river, saying, "Well, I don't need that."

Bob's murder affected us all. I can't imagine what it did to his wife and kids.

FROM THE GAME WARDEN'S CAMPFIRE

Dad

I had a few stories about my dad in my previous book. He was the reason I became a game warden. A true outdoorsman is how I would describe him. He taught me many things growing up. We often fished in secluded streams, and rarely did we ever miss hunting on the opening morning of squirrel season.

Dad loved to eat fish. However, he would not allow me to fillet the fish. To him, that was wasting too much good meat. While I didn't particularly appreciate eating around the bones, my father would have a massive pile of fish bones beside his plate after the meal. So, my regular job was cleaning the fish while using a clawed tool to get the scales off. I removed many fish scales. Dad would take a sharp knife and do the rest. He saved all the fish eggs since he ate those the same as the fish. I imagine all who grew up during the Great Depression did the same.

I always knew my father thoroughly enjoyed every fishing trip, whether we came home with fish or not. Still, somehow, I had started thinking it was all about catching a good number of fish. I remember the day I finally figured out it was something else entirely.

Not long after I landed the game warden job, I started receiving all the routine information that came with it. One thing I was accessing was a monthly schedule of rainbow trout stockings. Whenever possible, I needed to meet the trout truck when they stocked rainbows in two of my streams.

The public could also access this information from our department. This access meant a group usually waited at the streams on those days. More than a few fishermen could catch their limit of rainbow trout if they showed up on the stocking day.

Now, I would always know in advance when the trout were released. I thought Dad would be excited to be there, joining the others and catching his limit of rainbows on each one of these days. All this insider information would be great for us. So, I stopped by to ask my father if he'd like to join me for some fishing on stocking day. His reply was a simple "no."

I knew he loved to fish and eat trout, so I was puzzled why he wouldn't want to come to this. Men like my father were the old-school, no-nonsense type. With them, you should drop the subject entirely once you get your answer. This time, however, I respectfully ventured out and asked him, "Why not?" He replied, "Because I don't like fishing from the third row back." He was referring to fishing around the group of people who would be there. Dad always knew how to make his point.

After this, I fully realized it wasn't about catching fish. It was something way more than that to him. Being in the woods alone was an experience where he appreciated the One who created it. He liked getting away from everyone during times like these. I'm thankful I was able to come along often.

One night, Dad "made his point" to my brother. We were fishing for catfish at Sportsmen's Lake in Simpson County. My brother and I were in a small boat on the water while Dad sat alone in the dark on the lake's dam. Suddenly, a group of coyotes started howling nearby. It alarmed my brother, who yelled to the bank, "Dad, do you want us to come to get you in this boat?" He thought our father would be safer on the water. A voice in the dark whispered back, "No, I want you to shut up so I can hear the music." He always enjoyed sitting alone in the dark, listening to the owls and coyotes.

My father's first name was Spencer, but he went by his "Sol" Finn nickname. The Finns made sure everyone had a handle. Sol and Eva Finn had five children: Judy, Julian, Janine, Janelle, and Jeff. My dad called those five Dudes, Mugs, Neney, Blame Young'un (or Tooter,) and Hot Rod. He called himself a "country barn carpenter." He came from a long line of barn builders.

Dad would hire a group of workers who helped him construct barns. When I was growing up, Dad's crew consisted of two or three men who had substantial problems with alcohol. My father would give them their paycheck on Friday afternoon at the end of each week. By that time, they had already been penniless for days.

They would immediately take their paycheck, buy alcohol, and then go out "on a drunk" for the weekend. When Monday morning rolled around, the hangovers were now calling the shots. Dad was constantly upset that he couldn't round up a crew to work on Mondays.

In the early '70s, this all changed when a group of hippies bought some property in Allen County, Kentucky, and started the "Flying Frog Farm" commune. Some local rural people didn't want to hire these "wild" hippies. My father never judged anyone by their looks and had no problem hiring a group of long-haired young men.

He found them to be good carpenters. He didn't know or care what they did over the weekend. Whatever it was, it didn't give them a hangover on Monday mornings. So, my dad was finally happy to have a complete working crew every Monday.

One day, while building a barn, Dad got a hint about their weekend activity. One hippy on the top of a barn leaned over, and a small metal pipe fell out of his pocket. It dropped down on the ground at Dad's feet. My father picked up the smoker's apparatus while watching a young man fly down from the barn roof at lightning speed. My dad handed the pipe to him, saying, "You don't smoke, so what do you use in this?" His worker said, "Oh, Mr. Finn, you'd be surprised," and quickly climbed back up to the top of the barn.

On another day, those from the commune asked my father to come over and teach them. They knew he was an outdoorsman with years of knowledge. Dad would often dig ginseng and other plants in the woods like "Yellow Root." The hippies wanted to learn about these plants. So, one day, my father took a large group for a "plant and tree identification" walk in the woods.

After my father showed and described the leaves of the ginseng plant, one hippy named Al picked a plant and brought it over, asking if it was ginseng. Dad said, "No, Al, that is poison oak." He quickly dropped that plant.

When I was young, my father was a bird hunter. Being a "bird hunter" meant you had bird dogs and hunted quail. Dad kept several bird dogs over the years, but his all-time favorite was his beloved Ginger. She was an English Setter with ginger-colored spots. Money couldn't buy this dog. A few other hunters had offered cash to purchase her, but Dad turned them down. He wasn't going to part with Ginger.

There came a horrible day once when Ginger disappeared. My father was distraught, looking everywhere for her. He couldn't find her anywhere. After days of not locating her, my father did something surprising. He decided to see a fortune teller.

I want nothing to do with a fortune teller. I sincerely doubt my father wanted anything to do with one, either. But a bird hunter's love for his favorite dog caused my dad to do something out of the norm. So, he asked the fortune teller if she could tell him anything about finding his dog.

The fortune teller did whatever mediums do, and then she told my father this. "You won't find her now, but you will find her. You will get her from a woman in a blue housecoat with curlers in her hair." Well, as you can imagine, that frustrated my father, who left feeling it was all just a big waste of time.

A few weeks passed, and one morning, my mother got up and told my dad she had a dream about Ginger's whereabouts. She had dreamed his dog was over at another bird hunter's house. This hunter had offered Dad money for Ginger, and my father had turned him down. When Mom relayed her dream to him, he said, "Eva, get your coat. We're going there now".

I'm sure my mother was probably uneasy on the ride to this home, not knowing what my father would do or say. She told us about him walking up and knocking on their front door. The front door opened, and a woman in a blue housecoat with curlers in her hair stood there before him. My father said, "I've come for my dog."

As soon as my father spoke, Ginger heard his voice and started barking. His dog was tied to the bed inside the bedroom of this home. When he heard Ginger bark, he pushed the woman aside and walked straight to her bedroom, where he untied his dog. He cradled her in his arms and carried her out of the house, saying nothing to the woman at the door.

When my parents left the property, my mom (worried about what she had just witnessed) said, "Sol, you didn't say much to that lady." My father said, "Eva, if I had said anything to that woman, it would have been much worse than it was." Dad returned home with his Ginger and enjoyed many more hunting trips with her.

Some may wonder why I include stories of my father but not my mother. My father had a few rough edges. I guess his life gave me something to shoot for. My mother was a different story. I always felt Mother Teresa's life fell short of my mom's. I had no hopes of ever living up to that. All the injured stray cats, stray dogs, and stray people lost a true friend and resource on a stormy Halloween night when Eva Finn left this world.

Colorful Characters of the Past

I'll say things that many others won't. A few folks probably cringed when they heard I was writing books. They may feel some stories should die with us. I'm afraid I must disagree, and I will share a few of them in this chapter.

Many changes have taken place throughout the years in wildlife departments. Professionalism is stressed in law enforcement divisions these days. Years ago, there were many conservation officers already striving for professionalism. I worked with some fine men whom I highly respected. I also worked around a very few older guys I describe as colorful characters.

Like everyone else, when game wardens gather around a campfire, they tell stories. The truth may get stretched at times, and then some other times, possibly not.

The following are some tales about those few colorful character game wardens of the past. I could not verify the truth of these stories nor endorse any of these actions if they did occur. I will merely pass along some tales from the long-gone days of years past.

There was one game warden I would describe as the most famous of all the colorful characters. Legend had it this man got hired because they couldn't catch him breaking the game laws. A few claimed they gave him the wildlife officer job merely to get him to stop poaching. Doubtful as that is, this rumor got whispered by a few.

This man was a spirited jokester. I did find myself laughing at his antics whenever I was around him. Entertained or exasperated is how I would describe the officers who worked with him regularly.

One officer who worked with him told me this story. One Sunday morning, they worked together near a large public hunting area. It was during the gun season for deer. They were pulling over vehicles to monitor hunters and look for harvested deer. They were doing this roadblock style, and many hunters were driving through their road.

A small car pulled up to their roadblock. In it were two little, well-dressed elderly ladies on their way to church. While always taking advantage of an opportunity to be a practical jokester, our colorful character sprang into action and approached the car.

He had a heavy metal flashlight in his hand. It doubled as a police baton. He continuously flipped the flashlight and caught the other end while approaching the car. Seeing what was about to take place, the officer telling the story was already rolling his eyes and shaking his head.

Our spirited co-worker asked the elderly ladies, "What are you two girls up to today?" The quizzical and somewhat amused ladies said they were heading to church. While winking at his partner, he told the church ladies, "Let's have a look in that trunk." By now, his partner wanted to kill him but felt he better remain quiet and hope this would all end soon.

The little ladies got out and opened the trunk of their car. Our serious-acting prankster began his search. The elderly church ladies looked on as he moved things around, searching for some elusive dead deer.

By now, his partner wanted to wring his neck. With a sly smile and twinkle in his eye, he informed the elderly ladies they were good to go. I'm sure the Sunday school class had a good story that morning.

The guys who worked with him regularly could fill a book of entertaining tales, but I am betting they never will. I, however, will share the one legendary rumor about him that floated around the most.

The story goes that he had been catching some poachers spotlighting and killing deer. Each time he cited one, the judge would dismiss the charges in court and let them go. The game warden was furious at watching those he arrested getting turned loose. He decided it was time to do something about it.

They said one night, he drove out to the judge's farm. Taking a spotlight, he shined it into the windows of the house. After getting their attention with the light, he shined the spotlight on the judge's bull and shot it. He quickly took off before anyone could identify him.

After that night, they claimed this judge would throw the book at any poachers whenever he cited anyone for spotlighting. They said his court was the toughest on illegal night road hunters. The man behind the bench now hated anyone who shined spotlights and shot deer. (or bulls)

I doubt the bull shooting ever got confirmed, but if you knew this colorful character game warden, I'm sure you heard the legend of how he changed the weakest judge into the toughest one with a spotlight and a single rifle shot.

Another game warden I knew from the old days was a colorful character. I sometimes worked with him, which caused me to believe a few tales about him. They claimed that one night, he was trying to catch a group of raccoon hunters using a rifle during the closed season. Since some would run and try to hide the gun, this game warden hid behind a tree and waited for them to walk by him.

Several hunters were walking in a straight line. The game warden knew it was the last man in the group who had the rifle. So, he let all the others walk past him in the dark. When the last man with the gun walked past him, he stepped out behind him and grabbed him in a bear hug. The frightened hunter yelled to his friends, "Something's got me!"

Another time, this game warden was on a trout release stakeout. When the department truck released the rainbow trout in streams, a small crowd always gathered to fish for them. We often got complaints about some catching over their limit.

On these stakeouts, a game warden would hide in the bushes and observe to see how many trout different ones were catching. They would wear camouflage and watch with binoculars. Using a pad of paper and pencil, they would make notes.

The hidden game warden would radio his partner if he saw someone taking over the limit. This other wildlife officer had his truck stashed somewhere nearby. The one in the bushes would have his co-worker drive down and write them a citation. The game warden in the bushes was always supposed to remain hidden.

While hiding on the far side of the creek, this officer saw someone catching a limit of trout and then hiding the fish in the trunk of his car. He had started fishing again and was now catching more trout. There was no doubt he was over his daily limit.

Our game warden radioed his fellow officer to come to write this guy a ticket. When that officer arrived and accused the man of taking over the limit, the trout poacher got mad and started arguing. The conversation got heated. The trout poacher was now telling one lie after another.

The colorful character game warden hiding in the bushes had a temper. Hearing everything the poacher said, he couldn't stand it any longer. Up from the bushes, he jumped! While splashing straight across the creek and shaking his finger at the poacher, he blurted out, "You're a (bleep) liar, and your feet don't match!"

With the game warden's cover blown at that point, the trout poacher finally had to stop the lies. I had never heard that phrase before. We got many laughs out of it. I remember good times later, when game wardens heard someone telling lies, one officer would look at another one and say, "Their feet don't match."

This same officer sometimes would say things that other officers would only think. Hopefully, it was all talk. Either way, he knew how to get his point across.

Whenever an officer retired, his county of assignment would become vacant. After enough counties became vacant, the state would hire a group of brand-new officers. These new cadets would get sent off to training. After that, the ones in our area would come back here to start work in our district. We would all meet the new officers and begin working together. This exact procedure happened repeatedly until one day, we started hearing rumors that something unknown was happening.

There was a vacant county in our district. Rumors started surfacing, saying some unknown game warden was working in that county. There had been no new hires or cadet academies. There hadn't been any transfers either. All the officers in the district started wondering what was going on. The boss wouldn't answer any questions, so we were all left to wonder.

Some said this new man must be some covert officer. Others said he must be a federal agent. Then the whispers started that he was a "plant" who came here to spy on us. Whenever you tell employees nothing, they will try to fill in the blanks themselves, which usually turns ugly.

All of us tried to stay professional and keep our doubts to ourselves. That is all of us except for one colorful character with a temper.

When we finally did meet the mystery man, other officers welcomed him to our district. We all held our tongues about any of the rumors we had heard. But one guy was getting ready to tell him, "Your feet don't match." This time, however, he put it differently.

The new guy stuck out his hand to this older game warden. The older guy said, "It's good to meet you. If I ever catch you sneaking around my house, I have a metal culvert tile, a welder, and a backhoe. You'll be in that tile, and both ends welded shut and buried."

Later, the new officer left us as mysteriously as he came, but I'm sure he is still alive and not buried in a culvert tile somewhere. The older officer retired soon. All other new officers after that went through the cadet academy the same way we all had done.

One of the oldest colorful characters I met left me a present of sorts. I felt the word "cantankerous" was invented solely for this old guy.

Wildlife departments have problems with rumors. Many times, tales get spread about the department stocking dangerous animals. The more bizarre the story, the more some believe it is true.

One big rumor was that the department was stocking rattlesnakes to control the turkey population. Some claimed game wardens were dropping rattlesnakes from helicopters. There were all sorts of variations. Public relations crews did news releases trying to combat the wild rumors.

I'm a member of a few online game warden groups. When they talk among themselves, many joke about being a part of a clandestine black panther stocking club. Their humor, however, is kept to those who know how ridiculous it is. They know better than to say it to the public. Someone would take it and run with it. Someone else would say, "My uncle saw the game wardens stocking them!" From there, the snowball would just keep on rolling.

So, most professional officers know to do everything they can to stop any wild rumors of stocking bears, black panthers, or anything else. However, an older gentleman who is a cantankerous, colorful character will take a different approach to the problem.

Our old ornery game warden decided he would have a little fun with it. When asked if he had ever stocked rattlesnakes, he would say with a completely straight face, "Oh yes, I've done it often. We must trap them in the fall to keep them alive. Then I return them to Lake Malone and rerelease them each spring." I have little doubt he would have confirmed stocking black panthers or anything else if you asked him. To him, it was a fun pastime.

To those of us who came along after him, we constantly dealt with the fallout. Thankfully, he retired early, although I feel sure he still sat around the coffee shop somewhere with a twinkle in his eye, acting very serious while telling tall tales of stocking rattlesnakes.

No Stone Unturned

When I first became a game warden, I was learning the ropes working with Officer James Taylor in Warren County. His friends called him Jim.

Officer Taylor always stressed professionalism. When other game wardens hated wearing a tie with their uniform, you would rarely ever catch Jim without one.

Another officer also trained me. He took the opposite approach. He got upset if I showed up to work with him in a uniform. He preferred blue jeans and a flannel shirt with the badge in his pocket. He felt we could catch more violators that way. I understood both of their points of view and just tried to make my training officers happy.

Night-time poaching in the northern end of Warren County was constant. Jim was showing me the fine art of stopping spotlighters. (the Jim Taylor way)

He firmly believed that the first thing spotlighters should hear when getting pulled over is a 12-gauge pump shotgun racking a shell into the chamber. That sound set the mood music for the dance about to follow.

The warden believed it stopped any ideas of foolishness. So, each time we pulled over spotlighters, I jumped out of the passenger side and racked the 12-gauge loudly. They never reached for any guns after hearing that sound.

In those days, it was still legal to shine a spotlight looking for deer if you had no weapon. The law changed later, making it illegal whether you had a gun or not.

The counties on our district's end did not have many "lookers." That is what we called those who went spotlighting without a gun.

The other end of the district was different. Up there, the most popular entertainment at night was spotlighting to drive around and look at deer.

When we flew the airplane at night here, those in the air might find one "shining" every so often. Then, some officers on the ground would need directions to check them for guns.

I remember one night on the other end when the plane was flying over Webster and Henderson Counties. Instead of occasionally finding one spotlighter, the guys in the air said, "We have two shining over here and three others shining at different spots, then a couple more out further."

The teenagers must not have had a McDonald's to cruise around at night since they were all out spotlighting. It was more difficult catching the truly illegal ones with guns in those areas since we wasted so much time running down the "lookers."

At least in Warren County, we stayed alert. The chance that the spotlighters we stopped would have guns was high.

James and I found one bunch of spotlighters in northern Warren County. We were easing along the road in the dark with no lights. Officer Taylor already had his "night eyes." That was what we called the ability to see at night. Driving in the dark without lights was nothing to him. Since I was new, I couldn't see my hand before my face.

The truck we saw spotlighting was down in a big valley below us. My driver knew which way they were heading. He also knew he needed to drive fast to get them cut off before they got away.

We knew they would throw the gun away if he turned on his headlights. Many would toss the gun out the window to ditch the evidence of their crime.

While traveling faster in the dark, I looked straight down into a significant drop-off from my passenger side window. Way down below me were the spotlighters on another road. At this point, I felt the two tires on my side of the truck starting to go down into that drop-off. For a moment, I thought we might catch these poachers by falling out of the sky on top of them. Thankfully, Jim regained control, and we stayed on the high road.

We were able to keep them corralled and get them stopped. Taylor simultaneously hit them with a spotlight and blue lights. I watched two guys who had the deer in the headlights look as I stepped out to pump the 12-gauge loudly.

There was one other thing Officer James Taylor strongly believed. When searching spotlighters and their vehicles, he believed in leaving no stone unturned. Jim said he had heard of someone securing a long gun inside the bumper of their truck. Any place that could hide a rifle (or even a 25-automatic pistol) was about to be searched.

While assuming the position with both hands on the hood of our patrol truck, our two spotlighters were now trying to watch the game warden while he searched their vehicle for guns. One subject twisted his neck, trying to see each place being searched. My shotgun and I were monitoring them from the side.

Jim Taylor ensured there was no gun on any inch of this truck. After raising the hood, he spun the wingnut to remove the breather cap on the top above the engine. James had told me someone claimed they had hidden a small pistol in that compartment in the past.

My two interested parties had now started whispering to each other. One asked the other, "What is he doing now?" The other whispered, "He's taking the breather cap off." The first one said, "Why is he doing that?". The other shrugged his shoulders and replied, "Thorough, I guess."

I thought he guessed right. The game warden found no gun that night. I have no doubts it would have been discovered if one was there.

Well Imagine That

Poaching investigations will take you to strange places and introduce you to various people. You never know who you'll end up seeing. It's an eye-opening experience that could make you lose faith in humanity.

One day, I responded to a poaching call. This report was outside the area where I was assigned. It came from an adjoining county. I went and met with the landowner who reported it.

A few hours earlier, this landowner had observed a vehicle spotlighting around his farm in the middle of the night. He said they had shot a deer, then backed up into a small cemetery to stop and load the dead animal. The farmer got in his truck and went after them. They had their prize loaded and took off.

This landowner would not let them escape, so he gunned his engine and flew up behind them. He got a perfect description of the truck they were driving and saw their license plate number. This report was turning into one of those poaching investigations of my dreams. Later, that dream turned into a nightmare.

I quickly took statements from excellent witnesses. In the small cemetery, I collected evidence. I documented the deer's blood and hair from where the landowner said they threw the animal in the truck. A nice pair of sunglasses appeared to have fallen from the vehicle's passenger side during their hasty snatch and grab. So, I took photos and collected blood, hair, and sunglasses.

I had worked on lots of these cases, and this one felt like a slam dunk. Now, I would find and interview the two men the landowner had chased that night.

I ran a check on the license plate. My dispatcher said it belonged to a county official. The fact he was an official did not bother me. It only meant I'd knock on a door in a wealthier neighborhood. Whoever this was, they still needed to answer and be held accountable for their crimes.

I quickly drove by the official's house. The truck I wanted to see was missing. I was not too fond of this for one good reason. I needed to look in the bed of this truck when questioning this man. I gave it an hour or two, but my sought-after vehicle was not coming home.

Finally, I had to throw caution to the wind and knock on the door. Wherever that truck was, the driver would soon get a phone call. The minute I knocked on that door, I wanted to get to my poacher's truck fast.

A lovely lady in a nice home answered the door. I quickly got to the point and asked who drove the truck. She said it was her husband. I told her I needed to talk to him and asked where he was. She gave me a location, and (in my mind) the clock started ticking. I knew a phone call was taking place before I exited her driveway.

I was familiar with the place she gave me. It was a party spot for the affluent. I would be wasting no time getting there. In my mind, evidence was now disappearing at a rapid pace.

I wasn't driving; I was flying low to the house of entertainment. When I wheeled into the street, I had just missed a party. The men present had suddenly got the urge to have a truck-washing party. All the nice truck beds were exquisitely clean and dripping from the rinse water. (Imagine that)

I questioned the owner of the official truck. He claimed no one had borrowed his truck and that he was at home the night before. He swore he knew nothing about this. The truck's toolbox was a nice, distinctive one. I asked him, "What are the chances I already knew your truck with this plate number had this exact toolbox?" He replied, "I'm through talking."

I would have liked the truck to have deer blood and hair still coating the bed. Yet, driving away, I was feeling good about this case. I come from a county with a good legal system. The landowner had seen plenty, and I had good evidence and documentation. I knew my judge would have signed a criminal summons on this case. The other county's judge surely would also.

I prepared my case and presented it to the county attorney. I was very optimistic and felt like the prosecutor was, too. Then I got the news. The district judge ruled "not enough probable cause." I was stunned.

This landowner had seen plenty enough for this case. I had excellent evidence to go with it. How could he not allow me to put this poacher on trial?

This one ate at me for a long time. I approached my superiors. I wanted to appeal and go over this judge's head. It was not right. My bosses told me to leave it alone. They said these things happen, and you must move on.

I finally let it go. Yet I always wondered how that farmer felt after chasing them and seeing everything he saw. I moved on, but it stayed in the back of my mind. It bothered me that I couldn't help a landowner who cared as much as this farmer did. I never forgot about it.

Months later, the seasons had changed. It was springtime in Kentucky, and I was checking wild turkey hunters. I was on a back road in the same county where the deer poaching incident occurred. I observed a pair of turkey hunters coming out of a wooded lane in a truck. The vehicle had dark-tinted windows. I could barely see two men inside it. They were wearing camo.

I didn't want them trying to drive by me, so I used my vehicle to block the lane. Planning to check them, I wanted to see hunting licenses and turkey permits and then check their shotguns for plugs. If they had taken a turkey, I wanted to know if it had a legal tag.

While walking up to their vehicle, no one moved. Since no one stepped out and no windows rolled down, I assisted them by pulling open the driver's side door. There sat my two camo-clad wild turkey hunters. In the driver's seat, I was looking at the county official I had previously questioned for deer poaching. I remembered his face well from the "truck washing party."

You probably think I was staring a hole into this driver's face. But it was the passenger seat that had my full attention today. There sat the district judge who turned down my criminal summons on this man. Well, hello, your honor. (Fancy meeting you here.)

There was a good reason they didn't want to open a door or roll down a window. I checked my two hunters carefully. We exchanged some quiet looks, but no conversation was necessary. They had their licenses and tags.

I told them they were free to go because "evidently, I don't have enough probable cause" for anything else.

Following one longer look, I left.

Sometimes, when folks ask me now if I miss my job, I think back to this case and say, "Not too much."

I'll always wonder who poacher number two was in the spotlighter's truck that night. I don't have a glass slipper (or OJ's leather bloody glove), but I do have a really nice pair of sunglasses.

FROM THE GAME WARDEN'S CAMPFIRE

Backup on the Way

My county had high numbers of deer in the early days of being a game warden. Back then, some counties in the eastern part of the state had very few deer. When gun season rolled around, my department sometimes sent me help.

This help would be a game warden from eastern Kentucky sent here to work with me. The officers they brought down had only a few deer in their counties. Those officers always enjoyed getting to see all the nice bucks harvested here.

Whenever you travel to the opposite side of the state and encounter foreign terrain and different types of people, you sometimes pick up immediately what is taking place, then other times; it takes a while. The officers they sent were always willing to work and ready to do whatever was needed. They were brave, good men.

It was the opening weekend of gun season in November, and they had sent a good man to work with me. He was a big guy who was serious and dedicated to our profession. He was a new officer, but he was not a young officer. He had become a game warden later in life than most. We worked hard that weekend, and he entirely pulled his weight.

I had worked long enough to know the tricks poachers played. On opening weekend, their biggest "trick" revolved around getting your deer home without tagging it. There were many other violations, but for those wanting extra deer meat (or a chance at bigger antlers), not using your tag kept you in the game.

Whenever a hunter saw me coming, if fast movements started, it meant something. They usually tried to tag an untagged deer after getting that familiar "deer in the headlights look."

Some may have simply forgotten to do what was right. A game warden's appearance always reminds you of everything you should be doing.

Most of the ones I ran into didn't forget; with them, it was intentional. Regardless of motive, the law states tagging your deer is a must before moving the carcass.

This morning, my eastern Kentucky partner and I had already come across many deer hunters with lots of deer. We encountered a few violations and did our job accordingly. We stopped to check a deer camp after driving back a long, dead-end road. Both of us were out on foot, checking some hunters, when I looked up and saw something approaching.

A pickup drove up a small, paved road out of the river bottoms, and I saw men with guns in the back of the truck. I suspected the vehicle's bed was getting used as an elevated moving deer stand. I started walking down the paved road toward them.

It is illegal to hunt from a vehicle or a roadway. However, it wasn't unlawful for men to merely ride in the back of a truck with guns. So, I started walking to understand better what they were doing. I wanted to prove whether they were hunting from that truck bed.

The pickup stopped in the middle of the road when they saw me. I saw that familiar deer in the headlights look, followed by lots of fast movements. I immediately knew what was taking place.

Now I'm running down the center of a paved road, yelling, "STOP!"

I'm attempting to make them quit tagging deer by running and shouting. That should have occurred before loading the animals into the truck. I knew what they were doing. I understood them, and they understood me, although they weren't stopping. The more I yelled stop, the faster they went.

If some men saw a game warden in their sleep, they would probably start trying to tag something, just from a reflex reaction. It makes me wonder if some poor wife ever woke up with a tag attached to her and then said, "I guess my husband was dreaming about the game warden again last night."

So, I was running at them and yelling, "Stop!" While I was doing this, the one man who didn't understand what was taking place was my new partner. He had been working checking some hunters when he saw me running and yelling the word stop. This brave game warden saw a truck loaded with hunters and guns and heard me yelling at them. The next thing I know, he pulls his pistol out and runs straight at us.

Here, I have a bit of a predicament. I want some yahoos to quit tagging deer, while at the same time, I feel confident the brave officer behind me thinks they are trying to kill me. I wanted to communicate (before any bullets started flying) that these guys weren't scrambling for a gun; they were fumbling for a tag.

So now I'm trying to stop the bad guys in front of me while at the same time trying to stop the one good guy behind me.

I finally got them to stop tagging, and no shots got fired. I told my partner he could put his gun up and get his citation book out. One thing was for sure at this point. If some colossal crap ever hit the fan, I wouldn't have to worry whether this officer would be there backing me up. I had already seen that in action.

The Blue Light Specials

Whenever game wardens see someone with any part of a deer carcass in their vehicle, usually, blue lights come on, and the person gets pulled over and checked. During deer season, the blue lights got used with roadblocks to check for deer hunting or any other law violations. Whether pulling over moving traffic or working roadblocks, you always ran into some interesting things when the blue lights came on. Below are a few of those that I remember.

One Sunday of the opening weekend, I was pulling over a lot of vehicles heading home with harvested deer. Highway 68-80 in Logan County often appeared like the east-west migration route for eastern Kentucky deer hunters. I pulled over a truck with a small buck. Its antlers were tiny. I knew I would closely check this particular one on an opening weekend.

Deer hunters in Kentucky had one (and only one) antlered deer tag. Most prefer to avoid using that precious tag on a small buck early in the season. I needed to pay close attention whenever I saw small bucks on this day. Some took hammers, knocked off small racks, and then tagged the carcass with a doe tag.

This stop took place during the years of the adhesive permits. Hunters were supposed to cut a slit in the deer's leg and thread the tag through the slit. Then, they would peel each end back and firmly bond the two sticky ends. When done correctly, the permit would only come out after being destroyed.

We all stepped out and made small talk. "Looks like you've had some luck," I usually said. Then, it was time to check hunting licenses, identification, firearms, and deer tags. Everything looked good until I got to the leg of the small buck. When you've examined hundreds of these tags, you instinctively know if one seems different. This one did.

It appeared perfect. "Perfect" was not something I was used to seeing. I usually saw a lot of imperfections, and you could also throw in some blood, hair, grass, and anything else. When I reached down to feel the paper to see if the adhesive was working, it reminded me of an old song called "Slip Sliding Away."

Two adhesive sides will firmly glue together. One thing that won't glue together is Vaseline.

Vaseline will, however, give the appearance of being glued together. But you can also pull apart a Vaseline tag and reattach it to a more sought-after buck later. You can repeat that process as many times as you like. At times, I felt like poachers operated a hidden testing room where they all sat around trying to figure out how to beat this year's tagging process.

So, it was time for an exchange. The deer and the Vaseline-coated tag went with us as evidence, and in the place of those two things, the creative poacher received the pink copy of a citation to court.

During another deer season, I observed deer antlers in the back of a pickup. The antlers were poking through a plastic bag. This truck, however, was on Interstate 65 heading south. I would have to hurry to catch up before he entered Tennessee. I turned on the blue lights and stopped him before he reached the state line.

As I looked at the bag containing an antlered deer head and cape, the driver got out. He was from Alabama and heading home. He claimed this was not a Kentucky deer but one he had taken in Michigan. I told him, "No problem," our law stated he just needed to show me his Michigan license, tag, and confirmation.

At this point, his story started morphing.

On second thought, he hadn't taken this deer at all. It was his brother who took this deer. He said, "I'm just taking my brother's deer to Alabama to get it mounted." He claimed Alabama taxidermy rates were cheaper.

It rarely benefits you once you tell a game warden you killed a deer, change your mind, and say someone else killed it. (Just saying)

So, I started explaining that if he wanted to reach his sweet home in Alabama, he would have to show me his brother's license, tag, and confirmation. He had none of those either.

Finally, I informed him the buck's head was going with me as evidence, and I cited him for transporting wildlife parts without the proper permits. I told him he would have to come back to court in Kentucky in two weeks.

Two weeks later, my Alabama guy failed to show up for court. I had no authority to go to Alabama and arrest him; however, there was someone who did have arrest powers. The federal agent could charge him since this illegal deer had crossed state lines.

That agent contacted him and told him he had two choices. Choice one was to return to Kentucky and pay whatever fine the judge said. Choice two was to stay in Alabama until "You see my ugly face and then get lodged in a federal jail for a long time." He also said, "And one of those two will happen soon. Do you understand me, sweetheart?" The federal agent always had a way with words.

He must have understood the agent. He came back fast to Kentucky and paid his fine.

On one opening weekend, I had a group of game wardens come and join me. The blue lights were going at a roadblock, checking deer hunters heading home. Usually, we worked these roadblocks on Highway 68-80. It was the east-west corridor where most of my deer hunters from eastern Kentucky traveled. But on this day, we decided to try something new.

Adairville, Kentucky, is a small southern town near the state line. Highway 431 is the main road going through it, which will take you straight south into Tennessee. When leaving Adairville heading south, you go down a hill, curve, and cross a bridge over the South Fork of Red River. After that, you are less than a mile from the state line.

After crossing the bridge, the road opens into the river bottoms below. It was a nice roomy spot for a roadblock. The hunters leaving Adairville heading south could only see the roadblock once they crossed the bridge. You never want your roadblock seen from a long way off. Some will always turn around and make a run for it.

This day was the Sunday afternoon of deer season's opening weekend. It was peak time for some out-of-state hunters to be heading home. We wanted to check if they had taken any deer and had the proper non-resident license. Some would falsely purchase resident licenses to save money. Of course, you ran into other violations at these roadblocks.

We checked a few non-resident hunters leaving Kentucky and found several violations. Occasionally, we came across someone intoxicated. Some others would not have a driver's license, or there might be a warrant for their arrest.

So far, on this day, everything was running along routine, and then a small car came down the hill from Adairville.

When the driver of this car saw our blue lights, he immediately slowed down too early. There is a difference between slowing down for a roadblock and slowing down a long time before you get to it. Officers can tell if a driver is considering other options than coming through the roadblock.

There was nothing between the bridge and the roadblock except this one driveway to a farmhouse on the left. It was a long drive that paralleled the road where we were standing. The house sat just across the field and was reasonably close to us. This driveway was the one flaw in my plan, which gave an excellent con artist an excuse, and now I was looking at that superb con artist.

This little machine was a low, fast car from the city. The vehicle turned left into this drive and slowly started going to the farmhouse. It had the eyes of a whole group of game wardens focused on it. The car did not appear to belong at that farm or the man who got out of it. While playing it ever so cool, the guy approached the front door and started knocking.

By then, we were already talking. I knew we were observing a ruse. He was only pretending to visit to avoid coming through our roadblock. He had something to hide and did not want to be checked by us. Whoever he was, this man was a quick thinker and a good actor.

We usually kept one patrol vehicle facing the direction we would need to take off in case someone turned around and ran. That vehicle was positioned and ready. I then realized my plan's second flaw.

My good friend, Officer Tom Culton, would be driving that vehicle. He was a great officer, but my buddy sometimes thought and moved slowly. So, we were trying to get Tom to hurry up, get in his truck, and block that driveway. My pal felt he was playing it cool by going slow, but it was killing me while watching it. I knew this man would soon be making a run for it.

Our suspect pretended to knock on the front door of the house. Then he returned to his car and got in it before our officer entered his patrol unit. We started yelling, "Go, Tom, go!"

This time, the little car was no longer driving at the same speed on the farmer's driveway. Now, it was blasting off and only hitting on the high spots. Our game warden finally reached his truck and took off after him.

The little car was flying low, heading back into Adairville. This reckless driving was the last thing I wanted to see. I did not wish to have any high-speed pursuits, especially not in town. My friend Tom got his blue lights and sirens going but was having a rough time catching up to the speedster.

When the officer entered the city, some kids pointed and yelled, "He went that way!" The children were trying to help the game warden catch his fleeing suspect. But it was already too late. The little car had disappeared completely.

We caught several violators that day in the roadblock, but I'll always wonder about the one cool customer who got away.

FROM THE GAME WARDEN'S CAMPFIRE

Flying Fish

When I was a kid, my parents had an old set of the Encyclopedia Britannica. That was my Google back in the day. I usually looked through those oversized books to read about fish or wildlife. In one book, I saw a picture of a flying fish. Years later, on two separate occasions after becoming a game warden, I also saw flying fish, but these were slightly different.

Driving up Interstate 65 in the springtime should be uneventful for a wildlife officer. I was leaving Franklin, Kentucky, heading north to Bowling Green. While driving, I looked to the right and saw some men fishing at a farm pond. Pulling off the road, I intended to go over and check their fishing licenses.

They were all fishing on the right side of this pond. When I stopped, one man dropped his fishing rod and started running toward the left side as fast as possible. Whenever fishermen run, game wardens run also.

I was still determining where I was going; all I knew was I wanted to be wherever he was heading. My sprinting outdoorsman quickly reached the far side of the pond and grabbed a fish stringer in the grass. When he pulled it out of the water, I could see a lot of undersized fish.

They had more largemouth bass than the law allowed, and most were not the legal size. He hurriedly started shucking them off one at a time and throwing them into the air. Flying fish were raining down and smacking the top of the pond.

My feet ran as fast as they could while I yelled, "Stop!" The more I shouted for him to stop, the quicker he threw fish. I tried jumping over the interstate's fence and ripped my pants on the top string of barbed wire. I quickly realized the only thing that would make him stop throwing fish was me jerking that stringer out of his hands. So, with ripped pants, I continued running until I did exactly that.

When I reached him, quite a few undersized fish were still on the stringer. Thankfully, the gills of a fish don't slide off a nylon cord easily. I also cited him for failing to submit to a creel check and all the other charges.

The funny thing about this case was the thin green fish stringer on the far side of the large pond hiding in the tall grass would have never gotten noticed if he hadn't dropped his fishing rod and run to it. A guilty conscience will get you caught every time.

The second time I saw flying fish was a few years later. I was operating a boat on Boy Scout Lake in Russellville. My fellow game warden, Tom Culton, was in the boat with me. We were on a routine patrol checking fishing as we often did.

I had a problem checking fishing from the water on Boy Scout Lake. Back then, no one could use a gas engine on their boat except for the camp ranger and the game warden. All the fishermen had to use trolling motors only. They could not legally have a gas engine on their boat.

While the small gas engine helped me patrol the lake faster, it also served as an early warning system to law violators. They all assumed any boat coming down the lake with a gas engine was law enforcement.

I remember the first day I went to the lake with it. I started motoring across the large lake, heading toward the dam. At that time, I did not realize there were trails where people could walk to that area. They could hike in there and fish from the bank. The ones doing that hadn't seen a game warden in a long time.

Things started happening fast when my boat with the gas engine approached the far end. People were fishing on both ends of the dam. They immediately realized this was the game warden coming. What I saw next looked like two coveys of quail flushing from both sides as people ran in all directions. Most of those got away. That was when I realized there were pluses and minuses to the game warden being the only one with a gas engine.

On this day, while patrolling with my partner, I knew we would not have the element of surprise. We were making our way down the lake checking fishermen when I saw flying fish for the second time in my career. This time, undersized largemouth bass flew through the air after coming out of a boat's livewell.

I gunned my small gas engine as fast as it could go. My partner started yelling, "Stop throwing those fish!" Those words once again seemed to have the opposite desired results. Undersized largemouth bass flew even faster now. My friend looked around at me and blurted out, "Ram them!"

He knew the same thing I did. This guy would not stop throwing fish until a game warden slammed the door of the livewell shut. So, I went straight at them, hard and fast.

When our boats hit, Tom grabbed his hands and yelled, "Stop it!" Once again, I issued citations for the remaining undersized fish and for failing to allow a creel check. After that day, I started trying to patrol that lake with a trolling motor or hide and wait for them to come off the water before checking them.

Thankfully, those were the only two times I remember observing those flying fish.

Mr. Exceptional

Do you remember when the Associated Press ran the story about the Kentucky man who had taken a new world record Whitetail buck? It was quite the story. According to the national news agency, one of our fellow Kentucky hunters had traveled to Missouri and killed this new world-record deer. Later, there was one minor flaw in the AP's story. The Missouri Department of Conservation said it never happened.

Oh, there was a Kentucky man involved in that press release. Every so often, game wardens run into an individual they consider exceptional. The man I'm about to tell you about fits the bill and then some.

I am curious how he got the national news agency to carry the story about him setting a new world record. Undoubtedly, he was a smooth talker and teller of tall tales. In this, he excelled.

Sergeant Gerald Barnett and I started hearing talk of a deer hunter who was a gifted con artist. This individual hunted deer and attempted to lease ground around Todd and Logan Counties.

Here's the thing about a grifter of this caliber. During financial dealings of leasing lands from honest, hard-working farmers, a change takes place. Eventually, a guy like this is no longer the leasee; he becomes the lessor. Our entrepreneur is no longer just deer hunting; he's now making money.

Then comes his next logical step. If you can make money leasing out the farm you've leased, how much more can you make by leasing out other farms? Of course, you have no idea who owns those farms, but that's a trivial matter when you're a guy like this.

When you see a great hunting spot that some lucky hunter would love to pay good money to lease, it's a shame to let legalities stand in the way of making money. And when you're gifted enough to talk the Associated Press into running your new world record story, then talking a few excited deer hunters into leasing an excellent hunting spot (to which you have no legal right) is not a problem.

You get the picture.

This man did not live in our section of the state. A song says, "You'll never leave Harlan alive," but this exceptional guy had escaped Harlan County of eastern Kentucky, and somehow, we were unfortunate enough to inherit him.

When a man like this comes into your area to hunt, it's like having a problem bear with a tracking collar. You start getting reports of the trouble he has stirred up wherever he goes, but finally, his day arrives.

Sgt. Gerald Barnett was patrolling during deer season in Todd County. He stopped a van coming out of a field. The driver was the man we had been looking for, along with two other men.

The three men stepped out of the van. Our guy absolutely had the gift of gab, and very odd words immediately came out of his mouth.

According to scripture, the devil knows how to quote the bible. This guy had a gift for it, also. When his feet hit the ground, he started quoting bible verses. It was one of those odd "Silence of the Lambs" kind of moments.

The situation made the hair stand up on the back of the game warden's neck. Barnett immediately took precautions in case these three odd-acting men were planning to do harm.

Later, when searching the vehicle, the officer started finding large objects covered up underneath the van seats. Those items turned out to be four illegal deer carcasses underneath some quilts. Finally, charges were filed against the one stirring up so much trouble and his two friends.

Later, our talented grifter disappeared from our radar completely. We heard he got himself into some real trouble back in Harlan County. (imagine that) We hope he stayed in those deep, dark hills of eastern Kentucky.

FROM THE GAME WARDEN'S CAMPFIRE

The Daring Heist

The tenth commandment says you shall not covet. Some deer hunters struggle with that one when someone else takes a buck with a large rack. While they may wrestle with number ten, most will usually draw the line at commandment number eight, which states you shall not steal. That would be most, but not all.

Once again, it was deer season in Logan County, Kentucky. I was responding to the usual calls. The next call I got was a most unusual one. A Russellville City Police Detective was reporting a theft to a game warden. That should be the other way around, but this case was different.

The detective had legally harvested a nice large buck. He hung the trophy from a tree in his backyard. He was preparing to skin it. Before he got started, he needed to make a run somewhere. He lived in the city limits on a street with neighbors nearby.

While away on his errand, one of his neighbors looked out their window to see a strange truck backing into the detective's backyard. A guy jumped out, quickly cut down the hanging buck, loaded it into his truck, and took off. Yes, you heard that correctly. Someone stole a deer from a police detective's backyard with neighbors looking on.

This case came to me with some excellent witnesses and information. In no time at all, I knew who had done this. It was not the first time I had heard his name, but it was the only time I had heard of a daring deer heist like this.

I had already received calls and reports on this individual. People said he and a friend had been spotlighting and road hunting all over the northern end of my county. If their words were valid, he had already been trying hard to get that big buck illegally. It now appeared he had just stepped up his game.

I started the search for my brazen robber. He was lying low for a while, but I finally caught up to him. I read to him his legal rights and started to question him. There was little for me to ask. I knew what had happened due to some vigilant neighbors.

My subject had a question for me, making me pause and think. The inquiry was, "What will happen to me in court?" I was often asked that question and usually could give a good ballpark figure, but this time was different.

I had to tell him under normal conditions; I could answer that. I said, "But believe it or not, I've not had that many people drive across someone's backyard, cut down their deer from a tree, steal their buck, and take off with it."

I let him know I was a little stumped on this one. I then threw in a couple of extra words, "You're special."

I thought those last two words would get a rise out of him. It just seemed like the lights were on, but no one was home. I should have expected that from someone who stole a police detective's deer.

All the regular law enforcement activities followed. Deer season could always make a game warden shake his head.

Practical Jokes

When game wardens play practical jokes on each other, many times, those jokes involve wildlife. Years ago, the wildlife officer in Henderson County, Kentucky, was Sgt. William Eugene Cambron. To those who knew him, he was "Billy Gene." He was a big guy who kept a clean patrol truck. Back when many officers still smoked cigarettes in their vehicles, Sgt. Cambron posted a sign on the dash of his unit. The notice read, "No Smoking in this vehicle." He would be furious with anyone messing up his assigned property.

It was a cold January, and deer season was behind us. In those days, there was still a good number of trappers. The officers in our district were all coming to my assigned county. We were doing a joint trapping patrol in this area. While monitoring traplines, we would also check for any small game hunters. Logan County hadn't seen this many game warden trucks for a long time.

One of the officers working here that day was my friend Tom Culton. He was the wildlife officer in Muhlenberg County. Nothing would have made Tom happier than to pull a practical joke on Billy Gene Cambron if he didn't get caught. While walking along a creek bank checking a trapline, Officer Culton came across a frozen dead frog. Tom immediately knew what he wanted to do with that frog.

Inside Sgt. Cambron's clean truck, mounted on the dash by Velcro, was a thermal coffee mug with a lid. Billy Gene used to drink a lot of coffee from it but had cut back and wasn't using it often. Tom felt like that mug needed some use. Whenever you have a frozen dead frog in your pocket, you must time things just right to get it in the sergeant's coffee cup unnoticed.

Tom found his moment and completed his mission without getting caught. He wanted no one to know it was him who had done this. He knew the wrath that would follow. The dead frog went undetected for a long time. Later, Sgt. Cambron noticed a foul-smelling odor inside his clean patrol vehicle. He could not pinpoint the origin of the stench but decided a mouse must have gotten under his seat and died. Finally, the perplexed driver had had enough. One day, he took the entire seat out of the truck while searching for the dead rodent. Nothing he did seemed to help.

Above that "no smoking sign," air fresheners now hung from the rearview mirror. Finally, one day, he pulled loose the Velcro to get a coffee. Opening the lid, he beheld the source of his problem: a petrified leopard frog. Billy Gene's face was red on an average day, and I'm sure it glowed brighter than ever at that moment.

The angry sergeant was on an investigating mission for the next several weeks. He wanted to narrow it down to one person and find out who put the frog in his cup. Everyone denied responsibility. No one would admit to knowing who had done such a thing. At district meetings, Billy Gene seriously studied the faces of all the men he considered suspects. A more exhaustive law enforcement investigation has yet to happen.

One by one, he pinned down the possible perpetrators. After several confrontations, he felt he finally knew who had secreted the stinking amphibian into his airspace. A plan of revenge hatched in his brain.

If you knew my friend Tom Culton well, you knew he feared snakes. Once, I found the motherload of giant bullfrogs. It was where we could easily score a limit of large frog legs for the deep fryer. Tom was an excellent cook. We went after the frogs while planning our feast. While wading in the stream that night, many tiny common water snakes rose to the surface. They were not poisonous, so I got a kick from seeing them. My partner, however, was fear-stricken. I told him to ignore them and consider how good these frog legs would taste. Tom told me, "If one of those snakes swims up my pants leg, we'll eat peanut butter sandwiches."

Sgt. Cambron knew all about Tom's fear of snakes. He also knew if given a chance, Tom would get into your snacks and eat them. Combining those two pieces of information, Cambron concocted his get-even plan.

It was district meeting day. All officers in our district were looking sharp in full-dress uniforms. The captain sat at the head table in charge of the meeting. I usually sat near the end of one line of tables. Tom always sat in the middle of the same line.

Billy Gene usually sat at the opposite group of tables, but today, he had moved over to our side of the room. The sergeant had positioned himself directly across and in front of Tom. Cambron had brought a large box of chocolate-covered peanuts with him. Before the meeting started, he informed us all (except for Tom) that he had a live Garter snake inside this box of chocolates. He had planned this day for a while.

While the captain started giving us a rundown of the activity, Billy Gene pretended to eat a few treats from his box. Next, he laid the box on the table between him and Tom. Then he turned his chair around, facing away from his target while pretending to listen closely to the captain. The trap sat cocked and ready in front of his prey.

Officer Culton didn't take long to sneak in and grab the box of chocolates. While opening one end of the box quietly, all eyes were on him except for the big officer's eyes facing the other way. The unsuspecting candy thief, with one hand, gave the box a few good shakes, and several chocolate-covered peanuts fell out into his other hand. To our surprise, that was all that came out. He eased the box back into place while eating his stolen snake-flavored treats. No one said anything, and the meeting continued. After a while, Tom felt that Billy Gene would never know if a few more tasty chocolates went missing. So once again, he eased in close and snatched the box. After opening the lid, the peanuts stuck together, so he gave it a firmer shake this time.

In his open palm landed a quite lively Garter snake. The uniformed officer screamed like a little girl as his chair toppled over backward! The captain had to stop his meeting. Tom was doing a fast back-crawl away from some chocolate-covered peanuts. The candy was on the floor between his legs, with a small snake slithering around it. Sgt. Cambron then turned around, grinning big, and said, "That's for the frog in my cup." If you knew Billy Gene, you already know he threw in a few extra words.

The Jury Trial

Throughout my career, only a few cases ended up in an actual trial. Most got settled without going that far. If a trial did take place, they usually chose a hearing before the judge. I remember one case where the defendant requested one by a jury.

I knew a farmer who I considered to be an honest sportsman. He was a good man with a young family. One day, he called me upset over an incident that had taken place on his farm. He said wildlife laws got broken, so I went out and met with him to investigate. He relayed the following story to me.

On the previous evening, he was home with his family. Two men he knew who hunted raccoons had stopped by his house. They asked to run their hounds on his farm. He told them that would be fine. With his permission, they drove out to his property and started to hunt.

This evening was during the time of year when you could only train dogs. You couldn't shoot the raccoon. Having the rifle with you while hunting that night would have been illegal.

The farmer had a young son who wanted to learn about sportsmanship. That night, he and his son sat on the porch and listened to the coonhounds as they chased a raccoon. His son asked him what was happening, so he decided to teach him a few things about conservation.

He started by telling his son since this was springtime, the dogs could only chase the raccoons. He said the mothers were tending to their young now, so it would be illegal to kill one. If you shot a mother, all her babies would die. He added this is why we have season dates set.

The dogs were barking in the distance, and they could see the hunters' lights. Finally, the hounds had a raccoon up in a tree. The barks and howls were more serious now, and the light beams were searching around the top of a tree. The father told his young son, "Now they'll pull their dogs away from the tree and chase a different raccoon."

Seconds after saying those words, with lights still shining up into the tree, shots started firing. One of the two men was shooting while the other was shining the light. The dad, who was giving a conservation lesson, was furious.

I do not know everything that was said that night. I know the landowner was upset enough to give me a written statement the next day. I started my investigation for a violation of illegal hunting during the closed season.

I already knew both two men. Their names were mentioned to me quite often. The older retired game wardens from my area had already told me stories about the one. They claimed he had some fast feet. They said if you ever check him raccoon hunting, as soon as you say the words "game warden," he'll run like crazy.

The older officers said they knew this from experience. One claimed they had tried to catch him raccoon hunting illegally years ago. He had taken his young daughter with him that night. When they turned on their lights and said, "Game warden," they claimed his feet kicked into overdrive.

Soon, there was no trace of him. Only his little girl was standing alone in the woods now. The officers said they had to take the little girl home. After hearing this story, I had plenty of doubts I would ever catch him in the woods.

Now, with the landowner's statement, I thought he would finally face charges. I went and presented my case to the prosecuting attorney. After getting a summons against the two, my main suspect said he would not plead guilty and fight this in court.

The other man wanted no part in any court proceeding. He desired to enter a guilty plea and pay whatever fine the judge said. So, one paid his fine while the other requested a jury trial.

The day of our trial finally came. I entered the courthouse and spoke with the farmer and his young son, who were there to testify about what they saw and heard that night.

Our defendant approached me in the hallway before the proceedings started. He leaned in close and said, "You seem like a nice enough guy, but I'll tell you right now, when I get on that stand, I'm going to lie like a dog." I just shook my head and thought this should be quite a day.

A jury was selected, and we started our trial. The defendant testified, saying the farmer was mistaken. He admitted shots got fired that evening but claimed they occurred as they drove in on the farm. According to him, they saw a coyote, and it was still daylight enough, so one got out and shot at the coyote. He claimed it must have been their truck's headlights the landowner had seen. They were doing the landowner a favor by legally shooting a coyote during daylight hours. (According to him)

His testimony made the irate farmer ask a question to the court. He wanted to know, "When did coyotes start climbing trees?" According to the landowner, lights shone high into a tree when the shots went off.

Our trial finally ended after everyone got a chance to tell their story. The jury deliberated and, in this case, found the defendant "not guilty." The landowner was stunned.

After everyone else left the courtroom, the judge, me, the farmer, and his young son were the only ones remaining. The boy's father wanted to ask the judge to explain what happened here today to his son.

A caring judge sat down with a young boy in an almost empty courtroom to say, "Young man, I want you to know right doesn't always win. It didn't win here today, but you always tell the truth anyway."

Fast Eddie

Game wardens love bestowing nicknames on their fellow officers. In my day, the conservation officer in Hopkins County was Eddie Young. He picked up the handle of "Fast Eddie." Many times, that nickname got shortened to "Fast." Eddie faced some real hurdles during his early years as a game warden. There was a group of influential people who were out to get him. It seemed they would stop at nothing to get him fired or even worse. It all started one night when a young game warden was out patrolling to check for illegal hunting.

On this night, "Fast" heard some raccoon dogs barking. He started easing into the area quietly so he would be able to check any raccoon hunters. It was during the closed season. No one should be shooting out any raccoons this evening. They could, however, let their dogs chase and tree the raccoons. Game wardens often found what "should be" happening quite different from the reality of what was taking place.

Officer Young worked his way closer to the raccoon hunt. He exited his truck and saw lights shining up into a far-off tree. Hounds were bawling as he heard shots fired from a 22 rifle. Any doubts about this group being legal were now gone. Game wardens prefer to avoid getting spotted when approaching poachers. Unfortunately, things happen while driving in the dark with the headlights turned off. When Eddie thought luck was on his side tonight, his truck bottomed out in a muddy mess. His vehicle was now blocking the field road leading to these raccoon poachers.

He surveyed his situation to see if he could free his truck from the mire. Soon, headlights were approaching him from the field road ahead. His illegal poachers were now driving straight at him. His mired-up Chevy had the road blocked. The approaching truck stopped. Inside the vehicle were five men. It was an older man with his two sons and two grandsons. One of the two sons offered help to pull the truck out of the ditch. Eddie told them that would be nice and then pulled out a badge and identified himself as the game warden. Officer Young said, "The first thing we need to do is talk about that raccoon you just shot out."

(Here is the exact spot where things started going sideways.)

Any hopes of hearing an honest account of the recent raccoon hunting stopped. The truth quickly got tossed down into the mud, also. "We didn't shoot any raccoon," the driver exclaimed. The game warden sternly replied, "We both know that's a lie."

In the back of this poacher's truck were two things. There was a dog box full of tired coonhounds, and there was also a large toolbox. The game warden (believing the one contained a dead raccoon) said, "I'm going to see what's inside that toolbox." The driver exited the truck and exclaimed, "No, you're not! Not unless you have a search warrant." Officer Young said, "I don't need a search warrant to look in that box, and I'm fixing to see what you have in there."

At this moment in time, the passenger door of the poacher's truck flew open as his father took off running into the woods. The game warden felt sure the 22 rifle was also running out into the dark forest with the old man, never to be seen again. Eddie asked, "Where's he going?" The now cocky driver said, "Oh, he's probably just going to use the bathroom."

Determined to find some evidence of the crime, the officer stretched his hand out for the toolbox. The driver stepped to block him, saying, "You're not looking in there." The warden reached for the toolbox and said, "Yes, I am." As he put out his hand for the box, the driver hit his arm to knock him away.

Officer training for situations like this has changed quite a bit. In the early days of being a conservation officer, things were different. Eddie's mentor had told him what to do if someone ever hit him. That old game warden had told him to take his heavy flashlight and hit them back. His exact instructions were to wallop your aggressor hard on his left ear. The old guys believed fights got stopped when you busted them in the head. (Those fellows didn't play around.)

So, when the man hit Eddie's arm, he took the old game warden's advice. He drew back and swung hard for that left ear. The poacher moved as the flashlight came down. His movement made the blow land at the base of his neck on his shoulder. The weighted flashlight fell so hard it took the poacher down to his knees.

The wildlife officer opened the toolbox to find a freshly skinned, out-of-season raccoon pelt containing a 22-bullet hole. The wildlife officer was somewhat surprised at how fast they had skinned out their illegal take. He was expecting a dead carcass.

The man's father returned from his bathroom (gun-hiding) trip to the woods. He was mad that the game warden knocked down his son. The old man ran straight for the officer. Seeing he was about to be overpowered by five men, Eddie pulled out his revolver and told the grandfather to stay back. The son on the ground shouted, "Stay away, Dad! He's crazy! He'll shoot you!" The son had received an attitude adjustment. He didn't want his father to get shot over something he caused.

After this, the nonsense stopped. The wildlife officer arrested his attacker and charged the illegal poachers. Eddie then had someone call his dad and wake him up. He needed his father to come over with his tractor to pull his stuck Chevy out of the mud. After that, everything seemed fine as life returned to normal, but life as a game warden often teaches you everything is not as it seems.

It turned out that the man who hit the game warden and got arrested was a high-ranking official, and this man had a close friend who was an even higher-ranking official. These two men had worked together closely for years. As (bad) luck would have it, his powerful friend just happened to be someone of judicial and political importance. (Can you already see where this thing is going?)

Eddie's life seemed fine for a few days until a KY State Police detective visited him. The policeman hesitantly told the game warden he had a warrant for his arrest. Stunned, Eddie asked his fellow law enforcement officer, "You have a warrant for MY arrest?" The detective answered, "Yes, I'm afraid I do. Someone has told the prosecutor's office you are pulling guns on everyone and threatening everyone's life when you check them."

Eddie told him that was ridiculous. The trooper asked him to tell him what had happened. Officer Young relayed the story of the only night he had ever pulled out his gun and why. The detective slowly started understanding his warrant contained quite a bit of wrong information. The wise KSP investigator asked Eddie to give him the names of other raccoon hunters he had checked. He said he wanted to interview them first before serving this warrant.

So, he started questioning all the other hunters the game warden had checked. Each hunter told him there was no problem. They all said the wildlife officer had been entirely professional. The investigator was now detecting what was truly happening behind the scenes. What was going on was lies and plenty of them.

The arrest warrant got squashed. However, when you run into influential people who are used to getting their way (and they don't mind telling lies), you find you're not in a battle; you're in a war.

Rumors have always flowed freely regarding game wardens and hunting and fishing stories. I've often been shocked at what others said I did. In Officer Eddie Young's case, he now had powerful liars working behind the scenes trying to make the rumor mill destroy him. They wanted him fired and gone.

With the raccoon hunting case settled, other strange calls started getting reported. But bizarre reports often seem routine to game wardens.

Each time Eddie would respond to one of these calls, the powerful liars would go to work, trying their best to get him fired. On multiple occasions, Eddie would get out of bed to find the Department of Fish and Wildlife Commissioner and the law enforcement director in his driveway. Things constantly got blown out of proportion to the point that department heads from Frankfort were driving miles to pay the Hopkins County game warden a (non-friendly) visit to his home.

One of the cases involved an influential lady who had a pet fox. It was illegal to possess live wildlife without a permit. A check of the files showed no one in the area had a fox permit. A caller told the game warden each morning that this woman would come out of her house leading a live fox on a leash. The informant said she would attach the leash to a long wire stretched between two poles in her backyard. This way, the fox could run and play without escaping into the wild. (Which is precisely where the fox belonged.)

The wildlife officer drove by her house. Someone had stretched a wire across the backyard. He needed to see the fox to keep the informant out of this. So, he located a spot in the bushes where he could hide the following day and see if this was true. Right on time, out of the house, walked a lady with a Red Fox on a leash. She connected her lead to the wire, and the fox started to run and play. During times like these, you can see the true spirit of the animal and easily understand how wildlife needs to be in the wild.

The hidden game warden stepped out of the bushes and informed the lady he was seizing the illegal fox and citing her for the violation. Once again, manipulators twisted this story and tried to get Eddie fired for simply doing his job.

On another occasion, the wildlife officer's phone rang, and one furious woman had something to say. This caller was reporting a law violation. She claimed her husband had a lot of illegal, expensive waterfowl mounts. She wanted her husband prosecuted. Her reason was that she had caught him sleeping with her best friend. Furious was not a strong enough word for this lady.

When game wardens think about getting access to illegal mounts inside someone's home, we think about obtaining all the proper paperwork to make such seizures. None of that would be necessary this time. The caller said all these mounts could be easily located in her driveway. She had taken them all outside and beaten them severely with a baseball bat. (Did I mention she was mad?)

Once again, the game warden rounded up his evidence and cited someone, and once again, the powerful tried to tell stories, making the officer into the wrongdoer.

Another routine case got blown out of proportion when Officer Young received a report of a man possessing an illegal live bobcat. He correctly handled the case and ended up seizing the illegal feline. While driving home with a live bobcat in a cage, Eddie saw that his new state-issued patrol vehicle now needed fuel. He stopped at a gas station to fill up.

Rarely do game wardens appear in public areas without people approaching them to ask questions. It simply comes with the job. Tonight was no exception as a hunter approached the officer's truck with a question.

When this man saw a live bobcat in a cage, he got excited and called for his buddies to come and look. They, in turn, started calling for everyone else to gather and see the sight. After finally getting his truck topped off with fuel, Eddie could break free from the small crowd forming.

Later, the wildlife officer returned the cat to the wild. He took it to a vast wooded area. There was a sizeable cut soybean field nearby. After driving out into the dry field, he placed the cage in front of his truck.

Extremely gently, he eased open the container's door. Nothing happened. He thought he would sit in his vehicle for a few minutes to give it some time, so he took a few steps in that direction. Following a glance back, he saw an empty cage.

There was absolutely nothing any animal could hide behind in this open field. He looked around to see where the cat had gone. There was not a sign of anything in any direction. He had only taken his eyes off the cage for a second. A disappearing act like this was impossible. He started looking underneath his truck. The creature had evaporated into thin air.

Never doubt the speed of a bobcat.

Before long, official vehicles from the Frankfort office appeared in Officer Young's driveway. This time, the commissioner wanted to know why the Hopkins County Conservation Officer was carrying around a live bobcat in a cage to various public businesses and charging each person one dollar to come and view the wild animal. (I kid you not) Eddie was both dumbfounded and numb by this point in time. The lying brotherhood of callers made him sound like a traveling carnival barker yelling, "Come one! Come All! Step right up to see a live and vicious wild bobcat for just one single dollar!" The weary game warden once again had to prove what actually happened.

Here is where some other game wardens get added to Eddie's story. Most of the time, our fellow officers are there for us. We rely on them for help when we need it the most. But every once in a while, their "help" can be a little counterproductive.

Game wardens write tickets or make arrests when encountering those breaking wildlife laws. They usually use good personal judgment when doing this. I'm letting you in on a little secret here. Some officers believe a few wardens use their "good personal judgment" better in their home counties.

Since game wardens are state officers, they sometimes work in other counties outside their county of assignment. Guys have whispered a few times, "He wouldn't have written that citation in his home county where he would have to look those people in the face daily."

Whether that is true or not, occasionally, officers felt like their buddies lost some of their discretion when they left the home area. They felt like they had to deal with the fallout and repercussions while their citation-writing friend went home to sleep easy. So, like Eddie wasn't having enough problems on his own, now his "buddies" stepped in to (sort of) help him out.

The first bit of "help" came one night when two fellow game wardens were working in his county of assignment. These two officers were checking for illegal night hunting when they snuck up on a couple of men in a truck. This truck was coming down a road when its headlights shined into a field while turning a curve. In the area illuminated by the lights stood a raccoon.

The officers watched as the truck came to a stop. With the headlights still blinding the raccoon, the passenger door flew open and out jumped a goofball.

Game wardens are very familiar with goofballs. They encounter them regularly. Occasionally, though, you meet a guy who is truly special. This one appeared to be the leader of the goofball pack. Out in the field, he ran, barking and howling at the top of his lungs while doing his best coonhound impersonation.

Of course, the raccoon took off running with dumb (or dumber) chasing right after it, howling as he ran. After a few moments, the two-legged coonhound treed his prize in a small tree. I suppose the animal felt a small tree was good enough to escape this idiot.

However, our fun-loving jokester yelled to the truck, "Have you got anything I can knock him out with?" The driver yelled back, "The only thing I have is a rake." Our coondog wannabe shouted, "Bring it to me!"

So, the two game wardens stood hiding in the darkness and watched the driver enter the field with their weapon of opportunity. His frisky partner was still howling loudly and pawing at the tree. Soon, this pair swung the rake at the frightened animal until it finally fell from the small tree. Once again, the raccoon was on the run, with Bozo barking on its heels. Finally, it ran far enough and fast enough to leave this clown behind.

The wardens entered the field to make their presence known. The shoe was on the other foot now. The hunters had become the hunted, as the two embarrassed men asked, "Did you guys see us playing around with that raccoon?"

FROM THE GAME WARDEN'S CAMPFIRE

One of the officers said, "Oh yes, we saw it all. Now we need to see some identification." After that, the wildlife officers issued both men citations. On their tickets, the charge listed was "Attempting to take raccoon during the closed season with the aid of a garden rake."

Raccoon hunters know all about Kentucky's "shake out" season. Shaking a raccoon out of a tree during that season is legal. But since this was the closed season, these two received tickets.

Now, here is where I need to explain something. Officers from other counties can sometimes hurt you by helping you in these situations. Eddie was already fighting for his life, trying to save his career. Every wildlife citation written in his county was constantly put under the microscope. Now we had two numbskulls coming to court charged with garden rake crimes.

Moreover, lawyers and cops can develop a dark sense of humor. Eddie could picture himself walking into the courtroom with all of them grinning and shouting. "Everyone hide your garden rake! Here comes the game warden!"

Game wardens are used to being second-guessed on every decision they make. Picture a twelve-person jury hearing about a man barking at a raccoon and then knocking it out of a tree with a rake. Will some of them vote to find him guilty? (probably) Will some consider it ridiculous and a big waste of the court's time? (probably) Will the influential liars trying to get Eddie fired somehow attempt to use this to their benefit? (Absolutely)

Officer Young once again fought off the rumor mill. His two buddies, however, returned to his county and wrote one more citation. This next one took the cake.

It was the hunting season for rabbits. Some good-hearted soul decided to get a young man outdoors. This young man excelled at his school. He was the top student at the KY School for the Blind. (Any guesses about what happens next?)

The same two officers who cited the rake hunter now checked and gave a ticket to a young man who was legally blind. The charge listed was rabbit hunting without a license. If you thought malicious manipulators could put a spin on the human coonhound story, wait for them to get started on game wardens writing citations to blind kids.

These two officers claimed the young man was only partially blind and could see well enough to shoot a rabbit. Of course, that was quite different from how this story would get told.

Eddie was once again trying to fight his way out of controversy. Jokester lawyers and cops at the courthouse would laugh hilariously with their dark glasses and start tapping the floor with walking canes whenever the game warden stepped foot in the halls of justice.

The storm clouds hovered over Eddie's head time after time. The malicious liars did their best to manipulate the story whenever a wildlife citation was written. Divine intervention would be the only thing to stop this attack and save the game warden's career. Then, one day, somehow, the Good Lord showed up in the strangest form.

On a pretty spring day, Officer Eddie Young and his partner went out to check fishing licenses. At one point, his partner approached a man fishing at a small lake. He asked to see the man's fishing license. This guy looked at him and defiantly said, "God put these fish in this water. I don't need any little piece of paper to catch them!"

Eddie's partner told the angry man, "If you don't have a valid fishing license, I need to see some identification." The irate fisherman said, "I'm not giving you my name or anything else."

His partner asked Eddie, "What do we do when they refuse to tell who they are?" The game warden explained the legal procedures in a case like this. He said, "If he doesn't identify himself, you have no choice other than arresting him. We will have to figure out who he is at the jail." So that is what his partner did. Everything went routine after that.

Several days later, in the Frankfort office, the department's commissioner stepped foot in the assistant commissioner's office to tell him it was time to fire Eddie Young. He said those same people have called with another complaint, which sounds genuinely horrible. He said, "This officer has finally got to go."

The deputy commissioner asked what Eddie had done this time. His superior told him how terribly Eddie had treated a man at a particular lake. He said, "He never even asked to see a fishing license. He just threw handcuffs on this poor man and took him to jail."

It sounded like the game warden had been a real first-class jerk. The commissioner felt this all needed to stop once and for all.

His wise assistant asked what the fisherman's name was. After telling him who it was, the deputy commissioner said, "Yes, we are going to stop all of this completely now because it was not Eddie Young who arrested that man. That was me."

The Assistant Commissioner of the Dept. of Fish and Wildlife from the Frankfort office had decided to come down to Hopkins County and see for himself if Officer Young was as bad as the complaints said he was. This official had the same legal authority as a conservation officer, so he was Eddie's partner that day.

The dark conspiracy of liars had finally overplayed their hand. Now, it was crystal clear just how distorted their vindictive stories were. Someone above had stepped in and stopped a long-running corrupt vendetta.

Later, that assistant became the department's principal commissioner when his predecessor retired. His son became one of our conservation officers. It was good having a man in charge of our department who knew what walking in our boots was like. After all that, Fast Eddie Young finally returned to enjoying his life as a game warden.

I have always enjoyed working with Fast. I remember riding with him in Hopkins County one night in the middle of nowhere. Our entire district was again working with an airplane, looking for poachers.

Fourteen game wardens scattered and parked in snow-covered woods while two other officers got in a plane with a pilot. All the men were in Hopkins, Webster, and Henderson Counties.

We were out late during frigid weather, surrounded by high snow drifts. It seemed like the kind of night when any sensible man would be safely home with his family in a warm house, but we were never looking for sensible men.

Just when it appeared no one was out there, a voice from the airplane called on the radio, "We've got one." Those words usually meant they saw a vehicle using a spotlight. The officers in the air started directing game wardens on the ground. They told two officers where to drive to find this truck.

Pulling over vehicles with people shining a spotlight was something we did a lot. They were often just "lookers," a name we gave to those without a gun. However, everyone immediately knew this bunch would not be lookers.

First, it was later than usual. It was way past midnight. Secondly, it was freezing and dangerous outside. It was not a joy-riding type of night. But most importantly, it was the type of spotlight this bunch was shining.

This truck was shining with a red spotlight. In our career, we had all stopped dozens of vehicles without any guns while they shined a white spotlight. But I never remember any game warden stopping someone shining a red spotlight where there weren't loaded guns ready to use. These weren't deer poachers. These were fur poachers.

The red light will not frighten a fox, raccoon, mink, or other high-dollar fur-bearing animals. It gives the shooter more time for a good shot. Before this night, however, all the ones I knew of shining red spotlights were all doing it from a stopped position while calling foxes or from a boat on a secluded creek or river. These were the only ones I remember using a red light while traveling in a truck.

Our crew in the airplane started getting two game wardens in a truck closer to these outlaws. The officer in the air advised the ones on the ground to turn their headlights off. He said you guys are going to be driving up behind them. He wanted to get them close to the poachers before they knew what was happening.

Driving in the dark, my fellow officers could now see a truck up ahead and could see a red light bouncing off the fields and trees around it. They accelerated to close the gap between them. Soon, they would be right on top of them, hitting them with headlights and blue lights. But here is where something went wrong.

Before they could close the distance between the two trucks, our poachers caught a glimpse of something shiny coming up behind them, and they certainly weren't waiting around to find out what it was. They gunned their engine and took off! The only red light shining now was two taillights getting smaller and smaller.

Then the game warden turned on all his lights and sirens and punched his gas pedal to the floor! The officers, however, had a problem. There was still a good amount of distance they needed to cover. At this same time, they started realizing they had other troubles.

The vehicle they were chasing was not old or slow junk. This machine was a big, fast new truck. I heard one of the officers on the radio say, "I think this is one of those new F-250 Fords." It was flying low! Our two officers behind it were losing ground instead of gaining it.

Fast poachers didn't make us lose hope tonight. They may have been flying low, but we had three guys flying high. Our officers in the sky kept their eyes trained on the speeding poachers and relayed to the game wardens on the ground, which turns to make. A big engine and speed would not allow these poachers to escape tonight. So, for a while, it seemed we would eventually bring these outlaws to justice, but here is where we hit one more snag.

When fast poachers on the ground realize game wardens somehow know what turns they made, even though they shouldn't be able to know that, occasionally, a light bulb comes on. (or, in this case, light bulbs turn off)

This cagey bunch who caught a glimpse of a game warden truck now realized those weren't the only game wardens watching them. They knew not only did a patrol with no lights sneak up behind them, but an airplane with no lights was flying up above them. At that time, the monkey saw, and the monkey did.

Our fast-moving outlaws turned their lights off. Airplanes are a great help to catch night poachers when they are using lights. But when outlaws go black, then not so much.

The distance and the darkness proved too much for us on that night. You would like to catch them all, but sometimes you simply live to fight another day. The red-light poachers in the fast truck got away.

On another evening, Eddie came to Logan County to work with me. He had heard about the illegal raccoon hunters I had been catching by following them in an unmarked car. He came down to join me for one of these patrols. We again set up at the church parking lot across from the convenience store in Lewisburg.

Soon, we saw a single raccoon hunter preparing to head out for a night of hunting. It was during the closed season, so it would be illegal for him to take a 22-caliber rifle. We planned to check him to see if he was using a gun.

I told Eddie I knew this man and considered him a friend. He had taken me turkey hunting. Nevertheless, he still needed to be checked the same as all the other hunters.

It was then my friend Fast came up with a plan. He said, "You just drop me off, and I'll check this one." I would have checked him and cited him if he was illegal. I had done this before when friends broke the law. But tonight, I took Eddie up on his offer and allowed him to check this hunter.

Eddie stuck a citation booklet into his waistband. He would be ready to write the ticket if the man hunted illegally. So, with that, two game wardens in a small car started following a man going raccoon hunting. When we finally saw the river bottoms where he intended to hunt, I eased off the road and let Officer Young out of the car. I drove off and waited for him to radio me when he finished.

After a while, I received the radio call. "Come and get me," Eddie said. I eased down a dark gravel road to find a man needing a ride back into town. It was a game warden holding a 22 rifle. He said the raccoon hunter took it well, which I had no doubts about. He knew he was in the wrong, but he had a young dog and wanted to shoot out a raccoon for it. It was the chance many raccoon hunters took.

One waterfowl season, I was working with Eddie again. We were in his home county. Hopkins County had large river bottoms, and we were checking duck and goose hunters. After working our way into one spot, we saw a hunting blind and some decoys. A few guys were hunting, so we walked in to check them.

Officer Young talked with the head guy while I played the "bird dog" role. I was looking around for any signs of violations. Eddie had already seen something he did not like. They were hunting in a cut cornfield. He could see evidence of more spillage than average during the harvest. Some minor spillage is typical in this type of farming operation. Federal waterfall regulations carefully detailed what made an illegal baited area.

While I was walking around, I could already hear a disagreement starting up. Officer Young felt the spillage was too much, making it a baited area. The hunter argued the spillage was the average amount. I decided to walk out through the large plastic goose decoys. I saw something that would help Eddie to win his argument. I eased over and told him about it.

Eddie asked the man, "When did you cut this corn?" The man told him about how many weeks ago it happened. Eddie asked, "When did you put your goose decoys out?" The man told him it was a few days ago. Eddie then smiled and asked him how a corn picker sprayed loose-shelled corn several weeks ago on the backs of plastic goose decoys placed in the field a few days ago. They threw in the towel after that.

Then Eddie went over and started taking pictures of goose decoys with corn on their backs. We wrote several citations for waterfowl hunting in an illegally baited area.

All game wardens face difficulty when people possess wildlife as pets. They often do so illegally, but some get their permits and try the legal route. I usually wanted to discourage it simply from all the problems that arose. You don't have to be Siegfried & Roy or the Tiger King to discover the dangers.

Officer Eddie Young tried to warn one woman who wouldn't listen. Later, she had some deep regrets and the scars to prove it.

In a Walt Disney world, some grow up trusting wildlife to be like the cartoons. Any animal they raise from a baby must be good-natured and gentle. That thinking has a flaw; eventually, wildlife will point that out to you. It will hurt.

A lady in Hopkins County raised a pet deer. Frankly, I have a slight facial tick whenever I say the words "pet deer."

My experiences with the little sweethearts raised as pets consisted of my phone ringing a lot. I would answer it to hear about someone's rose bushes getting eaten and their children being in danger.

Then, I would call and get hold of the wildlife biologist with the dart gun. He would ask if we could get the deer confined in a shed or something. We never could accomplish that, so the biologist and I would go out there anyway.

He would then tell me how much these darts cost. If we could find the pet deer, we would shoot it. I can promise you they do not fall over immediately.

They will, however, completely disappear before going to sleep. They will go far enough that you can't find them. When they wake, they will (without a doubt) lose the expensive dart. The biologist will remind you again how much that thing cost, which was why he wanted the deer trapped in a shed from the start.

The next day, the pet deer would return to the house, eating another rose bush, and my phone would ring again.

Officer Eddie Young's incident occurred when a few people had legal permits to possess a live whitetail. The woman in his area felt the deer was safe for several reasons. She had raised it from being a baby and always treated it kindly. Plus, this deer was a female. So, in her mind, it would never grow antlers or get rowdy. (I bet you can't guess what she named it.)

So, anyway, she told the game warden not to worry about her beloved Bambi. Daily, she fed, watered, and petted it; there was no way Bambi would ever hurt her. Eddie tried to explain that was not the case, but his admonishments went nowhere.

And then, one day, the phone call finally came. The game warden heard a frail, faint voice asking, "Eddie, please come out and shoot Bambi. She tried to kill me."

On a day just like any other, she had gone out into her backyard to feed and water her pet. However, this time, something signaled that profound inner wild nature. The doe stood up on its two hind feet, and then, using the front two sharp hooves, came slamming down on her, knocking her down on the road. And Bambi didn't stop there.

The adult deer continued doing the same thing for a while, almost killing the lady before she finally crawled to safety.

Whether you want a selfie with a buffalo in Yellowstone, a pet doe, or something else, you too can become a great example of what not to do in a game warden story.

My last Fast Eddie story is this one, and it's a dilly. This story was legendary among the game wardens in our area of the state. It was more of a cautionary legend.

There was a night when four game wardens got together to go chase poachers. It was still in our early years. This period meant there were yet to be department vehicles. Everyone was still driving their personal cars or trucks.

Officer Young and another game warden patrolled while using Eddie's Chevrolet truck that night. The two other game wardens got into a big old Chevrolet car. They drove into massive bottoms where poachers had been spotlighting and killing deer.

Several different roads ran through these bottoms. They split up and hid their vehicles on opposite sides to watch and wait for poachers. A spotlight's bright flash rose into the air sometime during the night. The light's quick movement allowed all game wardens to realize their poachers had arrived. Headlights can't move as fast as a handheld spotlight, so it is easy to tell the difference.

Even though they were all in the same massive bottoms, the poachers weren't close to either set of officers. Both groups started up their vehicles and started getting closer to the poachers.

You have heard me say that game wardens only like to make their presence known at the last moment before catching a poacher. So, both vehicles eased through the darkness with no lights. Four sets of eyes watched the bright spotlight as it came up and then flashed back down.

Both sets of officers started driving faster to catch these outlaws. While hustling to catch up with these poachers, a colossal explosion stopped everything. All four game wardens went from looking at the night sky to seeing different stars in a thunderous BOOM!

In the first story I told about Eddie, I said, unfortunately, "things happen" when driving in the dark with your lights off. When two vehicles run to the same poachers, those "things" can worsen substantially.

The two wildlife officers in Eddie's Chevy truck had just crashed head-on into the front of the big Chevrolet car with the other two officers inside. All four game wardens were hurting and dazed as they crawled out of the wreckage. They searched for a working radio to try to call for help.

Help finally arrived to get the injured men to the hospital. Just as they loaded up to leave and get their injuries treated, off in the distance, a spotlight whipped around. A shot rang out from a poacher's rifle. Four injured game wardens just stood there looking. They knew more work was still out there waiting for them whenever they got mended and ready to chase poachers again. It somehow seemed like a fitting end to this catastrophic night.

Eddie arrived at the hospital with several pains. One of those pains he could quickly diagnose himself. Officer Young was hurting above his stomach. Opening his shirt, he was now a walking advertisement. Stamped in the center of his chest was a prominent Chevrolet logo. That outline from the middle of his steering wheel had impressively center-punched him. He carried it with him for days afterward.

The nurse asked him if he was having any other pains. Eddie replied, "The worst problem I have is a severe burning on top of my head." She looked up at the top of his head and started laughing. The giggling nurse said, "I guess so. Something has pulled all your hair out!"

The top center of Eddie's head had a large, seemingly shaved section, except the hair roots were also gone. His noggin had hit the truck's sun visor during the crash. Somehow, it had left him bald on top. The next day, he got to see his wrecked Chevy. When he flipped the sun visor down, all the hair from the top of his head fell in front of him. The game warden stood there looking at a pile of fallen hair. He was thankful he only got scalped and stamped on a night like that.

Cliff Hill Road

In 1987, when I moved up to Duncan Ridge in Logan County, Kentucky, I would have thought my road to be the most deserted stretch of backroad in several counties, but I was wrong.

Even though no one lived near me, and I could hear and see for miles, there was one road that was even rougher and more isolated. It was the next road over if you left my house hiking northwest.

Cliff Hill Road was just across the county line in Todd County. If you thought driving through my road was terrible, you just needed to try Cliff Hill. It was a (somewhat) gravel road that was hard to describe. It would help if you experienced it for yourself. If you came in a low-rider, you should plan to donate.

One night during deer season, several of us game wardens had been working together. It was late at night, and we decided to go home and quit chasing poachers for the evening. Sgt. Gerald Barnett and I left Lewisburg on HW 106 to head home. We were in separate vehicles, so I would turn off 106 onto Duncan Ridge Road and get home before Gerald. He lived near Guthrie, KY, in southern Todd County.

As he headed toward Elkton, I reached home and started to enter my back door. Just before it closed, I heard the familiar sound of a high-powered rifle shot. It appeared my night of chasing poachers was not over yet.

I turned to look toward the northwest, where I heard the blast. Rising over the dark woods and hills of Duncan Ridge were the quick flashes from a bright spotlight beam. There was no doubt about what was happening or where it was happening. Someone was spotlighting and shooting on Cliff Hill Road.

When I say Cliff Hill is the next road over, it sounds like a place I could get to fast. That was in no way the case. It wouldn't have been too far as the crow flies, but the way I had to drive to get over there left me with serious doubts about whether I could get there fast enough to catch them. I jumped back in my truck and took off quickly, hoping to reach this party before the last dance.

I flew to Antioch church and took a right. I zipped along Antioch Church Road until I reached Coal Bank Road in Todd County. Still, I was a long way from it. After several miles on Coal Bank Road, I was topping a rise to come down to Cliff Hill Road.

Before I could react and block the road, an old 4WD vehicle shot out of the gravel road. I quickly turned on my blue lights. My flashing blue lights made the poacher push his gas pedal to the floor. The race was on, and my truck was facing the wrong direction.

I was heading into Cliff Hill Road, and he was already on the pavement, driving hard and fast toward the Sharon Grove community. I turned around as quickly as possible, but it appeared he was gone. As my father would have said, that vehicle ran like a scalded dog. However, my escaping poachers traveling at a high rate of speed had one serious problem tonight.

When I left my house on Duncan Ridge Road, I radioed Sgt. Gerald Barnett and told him I was heading to poachers in his county. He was in Elkton, but he turned around fast to come back me up. When the poachers shot past me at the mouth of Cliff Hill Road, Barnett had already returned to the Sharon Grove store and was heading my way.

These low-flying criminals, thinking they were leaving law enforcement in their dust, were driving fast toward a game warden truck blocking the road with blue lights flashing and a 12-gauge shotgun pointing at them. The two men got past me but weren't getting past Barnett, at least not in one piece.

They soon had to come to a flying stop. The game warden ordered them out of the vehicle. These two were not happy campers. We took their guns and spotlight and charged them for attempting to elude. Later, we found a small buck deer they shot that night. We prosecuted them the same as all other poachers who tried to evade us.

Sometime after that, something much worse happened on Cliff Hill Road. Some said it was related to our case that night, but we never had proof.

In those days, bald eagles were only slowly returning to our area. I might see one a year during the wintertime. Golden eagles were even more scarce in Kentucky. I've been retired from the wildlife department for over a decade and have never seen a golden eagle in our state. However, back then, one came very close to my home without me knowing. That one got shot and killed on Cliff Hill Road.

One of the most majestic, rare birds around lost its life to a poacher on that deserted stretch of backroad. Some told us the crime was a payback to us for catching those poachers that night. We do not know if that is true or not. We never found any proof. The USFWS federal agent came to the Cliff Hill area for days searching for someone who killed the rare golden eagle, but that case remains unsolved.

Things Going Bump in the Night

It was a warm summer night around 2 AM, and I slept soundly. The phone rang, putting a stop to all that. Our dispatcher said there had been an accident on Lake Malone. He said I needed to hook my boat up and get there fast.

After quickly throwing on a uniform and hitching the boat trailer, I was speeding toward the lake. Dispatch said some fishermen had an accident, and their boat sank. They swam to a large rock in the water. The men were now sitting on this rock, waiting for me to rescue them. I hustled, not knowing their condition.

I arrived at the lake and got my boat launched. I motored to the spot described to me. I knew the exact location of the large rock.

Lake Malone was a pretty lake. I knew it all too well. It was the most beautiful place I always hated. I was constantly entering a hornet's nest of controversy there. Tonight, I would only be helping a few fishermen without encountering any other problems. (or so I thought) (you silly boy)

I located my wet, stranded guys. They were sitting on their rock; fortunately, no one was injured. Their boat was down, bubbling on the bottom of the lake. The sunken vessel would be a job for another day.

It's about 3 AM now, and I'm sitting in my patrol boat on a dark lake, talking to the guys on the rock. Boat traffic on the lake is next to nothing, but a large pontoon boat is soon motoring past us. Music is blaring from it. The craft heads on down the channel.

I started getting my refugees in my boat. I'm taking down information to fill out a boat accident report. During this time, the music blasting pontoon comes past us four times. I may not be the sharpest knife in the drawer, but I can already tell you I will have a problem with that pontoon boat tonight.

I get my poor stranded guys to safety. Now it is time to see what's behind door number two.

As much as I wanted to go home, sleep, and ignore that pontoon boat (and that was a lot), I knew I couldn't. If I did, I would soon get calls from Lake Malone saying no one can sleep because of some idiot playing loud music. What I expected to find was an intoxicated idiot. My expectations did not let me down.

Soon, I had blue lights on, pulling over a boat. On it was just one man. (one completely hammered man) This intoxicated gentleman had lost something. It was his house.

Of all the lovely lake cabins on Malone, he was so drunk he couldn't find the one where he lived. But evidently, he knew if he motored up and down the lake enough times (with music loud enough to wake the dead), then it would eventually dawn on him which house was his.

I knew exactly where he would sleep that night, so I was there to help.

It is tricky to arrest drunk boat operators on the water. You have a boat. They have a boat. They need handcuffs. You don't want to be known as that game warden who let a drunk, handcuffed man jump in the lake and drown.

If they fall out of a trooper's car, then they are a drunk, handcuffed man lying beside the road. If they fall out of my patrol vehicle, there are bubbles.

So, I got him arrested. With that matching bright orange life vest, I make his red face look pretty. (So hopefully no bubbles) I get the music turned off and start easing a pontoon boat to Shady Cliff dock while towing my patrol boat. I radioed my dispatcher, and two Logan County Sheriff's Deputies came to the lake to assist.

On my way to the dock, things are going reasonably well. The passenger has settled down, and any problems for the night may be over. (wishful thinking on my part)

My handcuffed buddy turned into a conversationalist. He wasn't saying anything that made sense, but was definitely talking. I nod and grunt as I steer toward my destination.

Pulling the large pontoon up to a dock near the boat ramp, I placed the gearshift into neutral. I then go to the front of the boat to tie it to the pier. I hear a familiar sound as I kneel, securing the vessel. It is the sound of a boat gearshift getting placed into gear. I turned around to see my passenger was no longer a passenger. He is once again a very drunk boat operator. Sitting in the captain's seat, he has placed the pontoon in reverse and now backs away from the dock.

I come close to getting knocked into the water as the unexpected and sudden change of direction occurs. I look up to see the welcome sight of two young Logan County Sheriff's Deputies running toward me. As I get up and wrestle the gear handle away from Captain Hardhead, the two young deputies grab him and make him airborne. He's a land lover now as they throw him out onto the Shady Cliff concrete boat ramp. They had seen his shenanigans and convinced him it was closing time. They hauled him off to jail, and I appreciated their assistance.

I retired over a decade ago. Occasionally, I eat lunch at the Shady Cliff Resort Restaurant. I sit there looking over the dock and the scenic lake, remembering all the happenings. There were fun times, too, but I'm still thankful the Good Lord allowed me this period of life to see Lake Malone from a new and better perspective.

The Poacher's Secret Weapon

After being a KY game warden for three years, I transferred to Logan County. I was still learning about the people in my new area. It was the night before the opening day of gun season for deer in November. I received a call that someone was already opening the firearm season early.

The caller advised a man was shooting deer as it was getting dark. I put out a radio call to Sgt. Gerald Barnett. He headed my way to come back me up as we headed to the north-center tip of my county.

The evening before rifle season was like the night before Christmas for kids. There was a lot of excitement in the air. There was also a lot of beer flowing in a few places and possibly a little whiskey.

Back then, deer camps were everywhere. My caller advised someone had shot a small buck on the farm beside him. He said they also had a deer camp over there. So now it was just after dark, as Sgt. Barnett and I headed to that camp.

I knew the farmer who owned this property. He had been having crop damage from a large number of deer. I had issued him some crop damage tags and was now getting ready to go on his property to look for one of his hunters.

This hunter had shot one of those problem deer. Even though this was illegal, he was helping out the farmer. The landowner was a big man, and I was a little nervous about how he would feel about us being there.

After locating the dead deer with the bullet hole, the informant told us which way the poacher traveled when he left. We were now heading in that same direction, entering a large deer camp.

Getting right to the point after making our introductions, we wanted to know who shot the deer. Of course, at first, no one admitted to knowing anything.

Over the years, I often found myself in a deer camp looking for that one jerk who had done something stupid. When asking questions, I saw a lot of shoulder shrugging. An old song mentioned looking for a diamond ring at the lost and found in a border town. I knew the feeling.

Having good evidence and some excellent leverage, we asked them if everyone in this camp wanted a citation. Since one guy had done this deed, it was time for our poacher to "fess up" and not get all his buddies in trouble.

Sgt. Barnett was addressing the crowd while I was searching for more evidence. Finally realizing the jig was up, one fine drunken gentleman came clean. He admitted it was him. He looked like a little old scruffy mountain man. His accent assured me he was from eastern Kentucky.

The tension finally started calming down in the camp. No one got accused of anything now since the little guy had already admitted it was him. It was one of those calm evenings where the fog lay low with no air stirring.

The other hunters settled around the campfire while I wrote a citation to our intoxicated friend. My sergeant was standing beside him, gathering information. We had no idea; even though we had seized his hunting rifle, our poacher still had one secret arsenal left. It was a weapon of mass destruction.

Earlier, he had loaded up on boiled eggs and brown beans when consuming all that beer. The little mountain man grinned as he silently discharged his weapon. While he showed the game warden his hunting license and deer tag in that still night air, I saw a look drift across my sergeant's face.

It appeared an invisible assailant had punched him square in the nose. His eyes started to tear up and water. Sgt. Barnett jumped backward into a combat stance, saying, "You little (bleep), you do that again, and I oughta to shoot you in your rear end!"

Our tiny poacher grinned even more as his toxic fumes spread through the air, taking out more casualties. The other hunters were now all cursing and running for cover.

Barnett backed up and started fanning his face and watering eyes. Choking, he said, "I should arrest you for this!" Later, I had never seen a happier man holding a court citation in his hand.

I then looked up to see the large landowner walking towards me. I was nervous and hoping I wouldn't have any problems with this man. The farmer leaned close to me and quietly said, "Jeff, I've never been so happy to see you in all my life. That little knucklehead has been driving me up the wall. He's never coming back here again. I don't care what you do to that rascal."

I was relieved to hear that. I've had a lot of respect for that man ever since. And I feel sure Barnett was glad the toxic sprayer never came back.

FROM THE GAME WARDEN'S CAMPFIRE

Traveling New Roads

A few times during my career, I encountered a touchy situation involving new roads. Whenever the state would start to build a new highway, they would buy up all the land and then bring in some large equipment to start work. As soon as they began marking the new area, some would realize the local landowner no longer had control. Those quick thinkers believed they could hunt on this ground now.

There were a lot of things wrong with this. First off, it was not a public hunting area. It was a road in the making.

The law said you had to obtain legal permission to hunt on any property. The state did not permit anyone to go hunting on work projects. A few even tried to get some shirt-tail relatives at the highway barn to write something on paper saying they could hunt game on the property. Plotter's schemes are endless.

Secondly, the adjoining landowners who sold this strip of property to the state usually had their farms posted. Some had run people off that ground for years.

Now, opportunistic trespassers felt they could hunt if they stayed on the far side of the state's orange ribbon. If you asked them, they would say, "It belongs to no one." A few said, "It belongs to all of us."

Of course, I looked at it differently. I would ask these hunters, "If state workers temporarily closed a two-mile section of road to work on it, can you legally run out there with your gun and start blasting?" To me, it was ridiculous. The absence of traffic does not turn a roadway into a public hunting area.

I can guarantee you one thing. Anytime these hopeful shooters started blasting from a new road in the making, the adjacent landowners would start ringing my phone. That was a proven fact.

I went through this process several times as new roads were built. My bosses and court officials would wade into it each time, offering their opinions. I always trudged on, happy when the new highway finished each time so all the controversy could finally stop.

The last section of road I remember getting formed brought the whole thing to a head. The earlier highways were built through wooded grounds where there was good deer hunting. Those landowners were upset about multiple high-powered rifles on a narrow strip of land nearby. This last road, however, was through open fields on the first of September.

Dove season mania was in full swing. Truckloads of hunters were all looking for a spot to shoot doves. Getting permission is always a problem, but this year, word spread about a new place where no one needed permission. An adjacent landowner had invested much money and labor on a legal wildlife food plot to develop an excellent dove hunt. (I'm sure you can see this coming.)

It was the perfect storm.

The opening of dove season was always a madhouse for game wardens. We would get sent to other counties to tackle the most significant violations. I was in one of those other counties when I got a call that a group of people in my county were all shooting from a new roadway and hunting on land without permission. Once again, I headed into a controversy where no one agreed on what was right.

This one, however, was different. It was in or near the city limits of Russellville, and someone had called the police. A police officer had showed up there first. He also waded in with his opinion of the legality of hunting from a new roadway. And when he started wading, he didn't stop in the shallow water.

Before transferring to Logan County, I worked in a connecting county. It was a small county, and I worked closely with several of the police. When cops get to know other cops, they talk and share stories. Knowing I was the wildlife officer, a few would admit things they had done in the past.

Some police officers are huge gun enthusiasts. I started learning that a tiny percentage of officers loved guns too much.

If some were working alone on the 3rd shift in a secluded area and a rabbit held still in their headlights, then the temptation to shoot a gun they loved got the best of them a few times. I knew a couple of those guys. They told me they had grown up and no longer did that. When I transferred to Logan County, I started hearing there was one here who possibly hadn't "grown up" yet.

Most police officers I worked with were great men. A few could be somewhat colorful characters. Before transferring, I had worked with several state troopers. They all seemed to be good guys who concentrated on their types of crime. In my new county, I met a state trooper I liked immediately. His name was Jerry Smith. I had heard about Trooper Smith checking fishing licenses by the bridge at Shady Cliff Boat Dock. I also heard about him catching some who were frog-gigging out of season. Jerry was a straight shooter who believed in enforcing all the state's laws. I have always enjoyed working with him.

I met another trooper who surprised me. That officer stuck out his hand to welcome me to the county. His first words were, "Don't mess with my fishing, and I won't mess with your driving, and I know you drive more than I fish." He just wanted to lay down some ground rules for the new game warden. I thought this might get interesting later.

There was one city police officer in particular who I knew loved guns a lot. I had heard a few of those late-night 3rd shift stories about him with rabbits in secluded spots. I might have to write a citation to a police officer. I hoped it wouldn't come to that, but it never left my mind, especially when I drove past the city park late at night.

Would you like to know what city police officer was working the day of the Dove shooting report? I'll give you three guesses; the first two don't count.

So anyway, my gun-nut cop gets a call saying people are shooting doves from the new roadway. He arrives and quickly decides there is nothing wrong with it. This officer was probably jealous he wasn't shooting at doves with these people. I mention this because it is precisely what he did.

FROM THE GAME WARDEN'S CAMPFIRE

One shooter asked the police officer if he thought it was illegal for them to hunt from this new roadway. The officer said, "Hand me your shotgun, and I'll show you what I think." He handed the policeman his shotgun and watched as the officer (in uniform) (on duty) swung around and shot at the next dove flying overhead.

I was mistaken if I thought the controversy of hunting from a new roadway couldn't get any worse.

When I returned to my county, the roadway dove hunt was gone. No one remained at the scene. I heard of what all took place from multiple sources. I am confident that everyone had many opinions about what I should or should not do in this situation.

And when I say everyone, that includes my immediate bosses, superior bosses, various political officials, adjacent landowner, other sportsmen, the county attorney, local police officers who liked this officer, local police officers who disliked this officer, along with the janitor at the courthouse.

Frankly, I was disgusted with the whole thing. As usual, I just wanted to try and do what was fair and proper. I planned to put some thought into it and do nothing rash.

Over the next day or so, while I was mulling things over, there were a lot of conversations around town about the cop who shot at the dove. I always preferred the peace of nature at my Duncan Ridge home over the gossipy corners of town. So, I wasn't hearing the talk and had no idea where it was all going.

The next thing I know, I'm getting a message from the office of the Chief of Police in Russellville. They asked me to come to their office to meet with the chief. I wanted to do that about as much as I wanted to go bull riding, but I cowboyed up and headed into town.

So, the game warden entered the city office building. An attractive, well-dressed lady escorted me back to the chief's office. The Russellville Chief of Police was sitting behind a beautiful large desk with his number two man in charge standing beside him. The two uniformed men asked me to come in and have a seat, and I did.

This whole thing was a no-win situation for me. Ultimately, I would be accused of wrongdoing no matter what I did or did not do. Being second-guessed is nothing new for a game warden, but the whole thing made me quieter than usual.

Some accused me of being a silent type of guy on a good day, and this certainly wasn't one of those. So, I just sat there waiting to see what they would say.

We started with just a few awkward moments. The best I can figure out is a few people were telling the chief that the game warden was getting ready to arrest one of his police officers. I could tell they were a little nervous. I wished Officer Trigger Happy had never put me in this situation. I imagined they were picturing headlines in the local paper, "Game Warden Arrests Police Officer." I was dreaming game warden goes fishing alone and forgets all this crap.

People have always told me I'm a calm type of guy. When faced with a predicament, I get even quieter while trying to figure it out. As a game warden, I noticed that when I got quiet, it made people nervous. It was not intentional. I simply needed a few moments to think.

Finally, the nervous chief broke the ice by saying, "Well, could you tell us your plans?" Since I had none of those, I simply said, "I just wish the cop hadn't shot at the dove."

With that statement, the chief came alive! In exasperation, he blurted out, "Jeff, believe me, we ALL wish the cop hadn't shot at the dove!"

The uniformed official beside him was shaking his head up and down vigorously. This situation weighed on more people than just me. I asked them, "Would it be alright if I don't charge the officer and just let you guys handle this?" It appeared I had handed them the winning lottery ticket.

Many will feel I should have charged the guy. I felt his bosses were relieved enough to act appropriately on the situation.

Since any violation had not occurred in my presence, the county attorney would have had to issue a criminal summons. I did not believe the county attorney would want to give a criminal summons for this.

The chief acting on this was the best way to go. Some will feel they swept things under the rug and that I should have done more. Whatever they did, thankfully, I never had any more problems like that.

FROM THE GAME WARDEN'S CAMPFIRE

We Got You Surrounded

I met a lot of young men who dreamed of becoming a game warden. I remember having those same dreams when the conservation officer came to my school and showed us films. For those who got the job, the first thing you did was to go through week after week of training classes. I attended this schooling back in 1983.

I stayed in our state's capital for several weeks during those days. An academy group of about 25 brand-new game wardens were being taught daily. Late one night, we also got some on-the-job training during a different class.

Some of the schooling for wildlife officers is getting trained with firearms. You are taken to the range and put through many scenarios. Since the goal is to get you well-versed in all life-like encounters, some weapon training takes place after dark. You will be dealing with poachers at night, so you must get familiar with that type of law enforcement.

Our firearms instructor sent us to the range one evening. The property, located on river bottoms, lay in some beautiful backcountry. You traveled down a ridge to reach these bottoms. We parked near the river while the instructor got the targets backed up against a hill. Any stray bullet had a great backstop there.

Lots of other shooters used this range. The locals around this area had become accustomed to hearing many gunshots. One man had become a little too comfortable on this night.

Our class group had been firing our weapons for a good while. We fired our 357 magnum pistols while bracing them on our heavy flashlights. The smell of burnt gunpowder drifted across the river bottoms like a layer of fog. During a pause, we all heard the bawl of a coonhound on top of the hill in front of us. Everyone laughed at the familiar sound.

Even though this was our training academy, we were all put to work immediately after being hired. We had already worked with other veteran game wardens checking raccoon hunting. So, listening to a raccoon dog barking at night and trying to plan the best way to check on the hunter was familiar to us.

The sound was, however, a thrilling thing to 25 new officers. We all looked at each other when someone said, "What are the odds they have a gun?" Everyone laughed again as someone else said, "Surely no one is that stupid."

Our training took place during the closed season. The raccoon hunters could allow their dogs to run, but it would be illegal for them to have a firearm with them tonight. Usually, they carried a 22-caliber rifle when attempting to shoot a raccoon.

We continued our training class, listening to dogs barking as they chased their prey. During every pause of our shots, a group of young game wardens tried to hear shots fired from a smaller caliber gun, and then finally, Bingo!

When the rifle on the hill started shooting, all heads snapped to look at our instructor. The man in charge said, "Well, boys, y'all are not going to let him poach a raccoon in front of 25 game wardens, are you?"

With that, it looked like someone had just released the starting gate at the Kentucky Derby. Everyone wanted to be the first game warden to catch the poacher with the gun.

Some of you reading this may think this must be one of those surprise training exercises. The kind where instructors get together, and someone pretends to be a poacher to see how young officers respond.

But this took place back in our early years of training. We were lucky even to have an instructor back then. We certainly did not have a team planning out surprise scenarios. No, this was just the world's unluckiest raccoon hunter.

Soon, the woods on top of that hill crawled with game wardens. Finding a man with some coonhounds and a rifle took very little time. One young officer seized the gun and came walking out with his prize.

Usually, that initial shock of getting caught by a game warden is the night's biggest shock for a violator. This poor guy, however, got quite a few more surprises as he started walking out.

He looked in one direction, and there were two more game wardens. He then glanced the other way, and there stood six more. After that, several different groups of officers started stepping out of the darkness.

He was beginning to feel like the Al Capone of raccoon hunters. His eyes got bigger each time another group of game wardens stepped out.

So, that night, a poacher got a citation. However, he also came away with a story that could always top any other told by his hunting buddies. Due to its embarrassing nature, I wonder if he ever told the tale of that night. I somehow bet he did.

One thing is for sure. The man made his way into my book. He may also be in the Guinness Book of World Records as the man caught by the most game wardens ever.

Lake Malone

I've struggled with this next chapter. When writing books, I only wanted to share stories that were either fun or exciting. I'm going to attempt to make this one interesting. You might skip this chapter if you prefer stories of game wardens chasing poachers. You simply can't be a conservation officer in Logan County, Kentucky, without including one chapter trying to describe law enforcement on Lake Malone.

I could tell you lots of stories about Malone. My department managed the 788-acre impoundment in Logan, Todd, and Muhlenberg Counties. The most significant number of houses on the lake were in Logan County, my assigned area. But being a state officer, I worked in all the others regularly.

To say we often ran into issues would be an understatement. To me, it was my own little private hornet's nest that I was required to go and shake each week.

Many people were packed in close together, sharing the same resource. It was a beautiful scenic area. At times, it also made me feel like a corrections officer at a minimum-security prison.

If I tried to list all the issues that arose, this book would be a novel. In all fairness, a lot of great folks lived around the lake. I made lifelong friends from some of those.

The regulations on horsepower restrictions and boat hull sizes have changed several times. There was a maximum length for the hulls, and the motor could not exceed 150 horsepower. I came across several vessels that were too long and cited those. The big challenge during all those years was what I called the "horsepower games."

Did you know a man with a 250-horsepower engine could get fake decals to cover it, saying it was a 150-horsepower engine?

Did you know you could falsify your official boat registration from the state to make it read 150 horsepower even though your motor was larger?

Did you know I could continue writing these same questions about liars and con artists for an extremely long time?

There is a church located back in my home county. Occasionally, I go there for a service. Each time I do, the pastor always introduces me from the pulpit. He then tells the congregation about a question he once had. He had asked me, "What would you do if I brought my over-horse-powered boat to Lake Malone?" He says, "Jeff Finn answered me and said pastor, I will write you a citation."

I was never entirely sure if he was bragging about me or scolding me, but either way, I was glad he performed his honest obligation from the pulpit and that I did mine when sitting in a boat on Lake Malone.

I do not know how many citations I wrote through the years for oversized horsepower, but it was a lot. Prominent warning signs posted at the boat ramps did little to stop it. My most memorable case of this violation came when a lady from Muhlenberg County bought a new ski boat.

FROM THE GAME WARDEN'S CAMPFIRE

The boat motor on this vessel had way more horsepower than 150. I stopped the boat on the water near the state park and issued her a citation. She was not a happy camper.

Someone had falsified the registration to make it read 150 horsepower. I took down all the information from this vessel and contacted the boat manufacturer.

When I first called them, the makers admitted the boat was considerably over horsepower. But when I requested documentation, the fun and games began.

I know you will find this hard to believe, but boat manufacturers who have received large amounts of money from wealthy clients do not like assisting law enforcement in prosecuting those buyers. Even when you send them legal subpoenas, the backroom outlaw shenanigans continue.

The president of this small company went on (what appeared to be) a permanent vacation and would no longer take a call from me. But if just one of my honest bass fishermen wanted to buy a 250-horsepower boat motor and didn't (because he wanted to be legal on Lake Malone), then I wasn't letting these crooks get away with this. I had other means to document proof for this case, so I prepared my evidence for our day in court.

Since I cited this lady on the Muhlenberg County end of the ski channel, I left my home area on court day and headed to Greenville, KY. The judge there opted for a pre-trial conference. I presented my documentation showing the boat motor was illegal for this lake. The lady showed her falsified records. The judge ruled he was dismissing the charges.

The woman looked at me and confidently said, "So now this thing is over." I calmly replied, "Oh no, we are far from over."

My remark angered her. She raised her voice as she pointed one finger at the prosecuting attorney, firmly stating, "If he says it's over, then it's over!" She forcefully told me I could do nothing the next time she brought her illegal boat to Lake Malone.

Once again, I calmly replied, "That is where you are wrong." I continued, "Only a small portion of the lake's ski channel is in Muhlenberg County. The next time you put that illegal boat on the lake, I will wait until you ski past the county line and cite you again. Then, you and I will do this same thing in Logan County before my judge."

My words made her head snap around to ask the county attorney, "Can he do that?" The court official said, "Yes he can."

That ended the conversation. There was no need to say more. I never ran into that boat on the lake again. My finger-pointing lady wanted to avoid coming to Russellville and standing before an honest judge with her forged paperwork.

The lake made me thankful for my court system. I often wanted to work only the Logan and Todd County portions of the water while staying out of the "free state of Muhlenberg," as they called it.

Also, for those who think I possibly have not heard the arguments of prop horsepower vs. engine horsepower or the installation of horsepower reduction devices that can be added (and later snuck back off), please trust me on this one thing. I've heard.

Jet Skis.

Just mentioning those two words usually causes a reaction.

Lake Malone was created for those who enjoyed fishing, but one channel was allowed to have a skiing season. When I became one of the game wardens on the lake, skiing or using Jet Skis was forbidden in the "fishing only" areas.

I continued informing the public the same way the older officers did. I told them anyone riding a Jet Ski is skiing. Therefore, you could not have a personal watercraft in the fishing areas. This strategy worked out well for a long time, allowing my fishermen to fish in peace.

After that, at one point, the game wardens and the water patrol officers merged to become one and the same. Following that merger, I was informed I could no longer keep Jet Skis out of the fishing areas. Now, the unhappy camper was me.

They claimed the water patrol had classified Jet Skis to be a boat, and they could legally go anywhere a boat could go. I thought this to be ridiculous and the end of peaceful fishing in my lake's "no ski" areas, but I had no choice. My bosses told me, "No one can do anything about this."

I knew some folks with cabins in the fishing areas who owned Jet Skis. I suspected they were behind this. They did not want to bother to trailer them and drive to the ramps in the ski channel.

Some of those had claimed that if we allowed them to run their Jet Skis on the water from their docks to the ski area, they would do that using idle speed only in the fishing area. (Insert belly laugh here) (Make it a big one.)

Anyone who thinks teenagers are the fastest and most reckless things on the water has never watched a sixty-something-year-old man on a Jet Ski. Nothing resurrects the idiotic thrills of youth in a senior citizen like sitting down on a Sea-Doo.

So soon after the change took place, allowing Jet Skis in the fishing areas on my lake (because they cannot legally regulate them out of anywhere a boat can go), our department opened up its newest body of water, Cedar Creek Lake.

If you open your fishing guide, you will see all the usual boat and marina regulations on this new reservoir. You will also notice these words, "Personal watercraft are prohibited on Cedar Creek Lake." (Now, picture my head exploding after reading those words.) Someone had told me that was impossible to do.

It's a funny thing about regulations. They change (and can be changed) based on who wants them to read differently. You try to do the best you can for the people you serve, but in the end, you have to march forward and go on.

My department learned some valuable lessons from Lake Malone. There are several different regulations on Cedar Creek Lake, which show me some past mistakes won't happen again.

During my early years on the lake, I was a game warden, nothing more, nothing less. That is the career I chose and what I wanted to be. If you got out on the lake back then, you might run into a wildlife officer in one boat and a water patrol officer in another. We were separated in those days and didn't work for the same agency.

I liked it that way. Back then, I did not check your boat registration, fire extinguisher, or life jacket, and I could have cared less if you were drinking a beer. I also did not work on boat accidents or drowning investigations. I had plenty to do monitoring, hunting, and fishing and I enjoyed concentrating on my wildlife enforcement job.

But like I said earlier, some decisions happen above your pay grade. So, these two separate law enforcement jobs were merged by the state. The sales pitch I heard for this merger was how good it would be for us since we would have all this extra help.

At that time, Officer Rick Minton was the water patrol officer in the big blue and white boat on the lake. So, the game wardens were told Rick will now be able to help you guys check fishing along with the many other duties you have. Well, that was the sales pitch anyway.

The actual outcome was this. I never saw Rick Minton on Lake Malone again after that day. He did not need to come to the lake anymore since I could and should do his job now.

All that help I was supposed to get changed me from being a wildlife officer 100% to 50% of the time. For the other 50%, I was now an areawide water patrol officer. I was told some other states had done this same thing. Some officers were happy about the merger. I just had to accept it.

Now that we were all supposed to be doing the same job, it was apparent some extra training needed to take place. I talked with a former water patrol guy about fishing regulations one day. When I mentioned several species, he stopped me and asked, "What's a shellcracker?"

He had been Kentucky's version of the state police on the water for some time, but now he was a game warden who didn't know one fish species from another. He had grown up to be a police officer and just wasn't the hunting or fishing type.

If you grew up with my dad, you knew a shellcracker and a blackperch by the time you were 12 years old. (That's a Redear Sunfish and Rock Bass if you didn't grow up in our area of Kentucky.)

But truthfully, I'm sure the water patrol officers were equally frustrated with me. I certainly didn't know how to look in someone's eyes to see if they had enough nystagmus to arrest them for drunk boat driving, and I wasn't looking forward to learning it. In a similar version, I probably asked one of those guys, "What's nystagmus?" After several training classes and some on-the-job training, everyone finally found their way.

In those days, I attended church with many people I considered friends. At one time, our church offered a night course of lessons on "Financial Peace" by Dave Ramsey. A good group of couples got together to take this class. We all got to make some good friends from those evenings together.

I got to know one couple in this class. The guy was usually quiet but funny. I enjoyed them both. Months later, I was out in my boat patrolling Lake Malone. While idling past the docks beside the Shady Cliff Motel, I saw this guy. He was sitting by the pool with a large group of family members. He appeared like he wanted to escape and wasn't that happy.

I knew that feeling, so I asked him if he wanted to ride on the water for a while. He jumped at the chance. I knew he had a boat and liked fishing on the lake, so we hung around a bit, discussing the best fishing spots. It was a good day for him and me.

Not long after that, I had to do the least favorite of my new water patrol duties. I had to search for the dead body of a drowning victim on Lake Malone. It was the same man who had ridden around with me that day.

Now that I was also the state water patrol officer, I had already worked on some drowning investigations. They were sad and time-consuming. The older water patrol officer had performed many of these. He was a great source of information.

If a body sank to the bottom, there were formulas for figuring out when it would float back up. The older officer gave me the best tip. He said, "Bodies float back up to the top when they want to come up." He was telling me the formulas do not work. He saw some bodies float back up fast while others stayed down for days, weeks, or months.

There is one thing I can tell you about being a game warden who is now a water patrol officer. If grieving family members come to the water daily, and possibly a TV news film crew, your bosses will require you to be there. Those cases will take priority over all wildlife patrols, poaching investigations, official meetings, or anything else.

My friend's body was not one of those that floated back up fast. His empty boat narrowed things down for me. Someone found the vessel motoring around in a circle with no driver. With that, I knew where to center my search on the lake.

So, day after day, and then week after week, I met with family members at the dock and then searched for the body of their loved one. Here is where I started realizing I had a whole new problem with this case.

All my other drowning cases were open and shut. Once, a young man fell off the wall of the Rochester dam while fishing on the Green River. I put my boat on that river daily while watching his grieving family members until we finally found him.

Another time, a few were camping out by Wolf Lick Creek. Some had a few too many drinks. The following day, one camper was missing. This case was a mystery at first to some. They were dragging the creek for a body but were not finding anything. Our canine officer brought his dog to track him and see if the man had wandered off. It seemed he had disappeared into thin air in the middle of the night.

Investigations have taught me to follow the evidence. If you slow down, think, and follow the clues, many times, things will become more evident. I walked around that campsite and counted many empty beer cans. A man who had consumed this much beer would not go far.

Since no vehicles were missing, if you figured the odds, our missing man went into that deep water sometime during the night. Wolf Lick had a high, muddy bank. From a lifetime of fishing and trapping streams with my father, I could quickly tell you what a creek bank would look like after you got into the water. Dad had me "reading sign" on banks like that when I was young. That is what he called it when we scoured the mud for disturbances and tracks.

So, while others were looking high and low for this man, I slowly and methodically started examining the creek bank around this campsite. Soon, I found two familiar-looking skid marks. I knew I was looking at the place where a late-night accident happened. After that, I was confident those dragging for a body would eventually find him, and they did. A steep, slick, muddy bank above a deep creek can get you killed when you're completely sober.

There were other drowning cases, but everyone always agreed on what happened. The family members knew it was just a horrible accident each time. My friend's case at Lake Malone was different. Everyone was certainly not in agreement there.

I would arrive at the lake with my boat each day to continue my search, always praying today is the day I find him. I would speak with the family members gathered around the state dock. Some drowning victims were found after just a few days. That was not the case here. Soon, I started hearing talk.

Grieving family members over a period of time can start having doubts about what happened. Some did not believe this was an accidental drowning. They had begun to think his wife had killed him and staged the scene. Each day, when I met with the family members, I could sense a division in the group.

I had gotten a feel for this couple when I attended those church group meetings. I came to know them both. I often get told that all people are the same. It is natural to think others must feel and react like we do. The longer I live, the less I agree with that thinking. I find some rather significant eye-opening differences in people.

Some family members were saying his wife was not reacting normally. Her reactions (or lack thereof) further fueled their belief she had him killed. I had already gotten to know this lady. I had seen her react to her quirky husband's spending habits during our "Financial Peace" course. Now, she was not responding any differently than she did back then. She reacted in her own kind of way, not the way you would think.

Still, investigators searching for a body should hear all the facts and leads. So, I listened respectfully to any family member who offered an opinion. But besides knowing this lady and her reactions, there was one rather large reason why I did not believe she had killed her husband.

You see, game wardens know a thing or two about empty boats motoring around in a circle by themselves. It is something you will run into more than once in your career. Trying to stop one of those boats can get you hurt or worse. Trying to make that happen on a secluded section of a lake to use as an alibi following a murder would take multiple people and some good planning.

An operation like that would also need to be followed by some good luck in not getting run over by an empty boat running wide open. It was simply too much to attempt. If you followed your evidence, it did not lead you there. The old water patrol officer told me to have patience. He said it sometimes takes months before a body returns to you. In this case, he was spot on.

Her husband's body finally returned to us in the lake. We found him not far from the location of his runaway boat. Those saying he was murdered and buried elsewhere finally had to admit they were wrong.

The fish and game department managed Lake Malone. It had one regulation that served as the constant burr in my saddle. In contrast, other officers would have considered this law a Godsend (and often did). On the other hand, I didn't particularly appreciate enforcing the "no wake" regulation when passing boats engaged in fishing.

It sounds so simple. You must use idle speed only when boating past someone fishing. While this law may seem black and white to some, I saw more than fifty shades of grey. (Way more)

Game wardens are routinely evaluated by their superiors. Nine law enforcement districts in Kentucky existed, with nine captains over those areas. When grading officers, one factor considered is the number of citations an officer writes. Some say it is the most important of all the factors. (They may not voice that openly.) (But if you know, you know.)

The "no wake" regulation did not list a distance. Since wakes travel across the top of the water, legally, you must idle past any boat engaged in fishing, no matter the distance between you and them.

If you want to write a citation, you can write them daily. One officer told me that any officer who works the "no wakes" on Lake Malone could be Kentucky's "Officer of the Year" every year. He felt like I had a gold mine. I looked at it differently.

Once, I did a test. I put on a full-dress uniform with a shiny badge. After placing the blue light on the front, I stood tall in my marked game warden patrol craft. I anchored beside some folks who were fishing in another boat. I then had several boats come by me while waving at me. While looking directly at me, knowing I was the game warden, they never slowed to idle speed. They were utterly clueless.

Some felt you should warn that type, the ones who didn't know. Others said you should cite them all if you write a ticket to one. There were plenty of opinions to go around.

It was rumored a few officers who had recently not written any citations would come to Lake Malone, where they could easily make up their needed numbers. Some said getting a "no wake" ticket on those days was effortless.

The giant Corp of Engineers lakes did not have this regulation. Those accustomed to boating on those bodies of water got a rude awakening when visiting Malone.

The controversy was never-ending. I thought I'd ask some of my fellow game wardens from the other department lakes how they handled this hot potato issue. After I asked them, I immediately regretted that.

Lake Beshear (another one of our department lakes) is a 760-acre reservoir in Caldwell and Christian counties in Kentucky. Those two counties are part of our first law enforcement district. Lake Malone's three counties are inside the adjoining second district. Each of the nine enforcement areas had its own captain and lieutenant.

The inside gossip line sometimes called these areas the nine separate kings and kingdoms. That was said when one district was handling something differently from another one. You could complain to the Frankfort office about how we should all be on the same page. The only one who usually got into trouble over those complaints was you. (Just saying)

Since I got frustrated with the "no wake" regulation on Lake Malone, I decided to ask the officers in the first district how they handled this monster issue on Lake Beshear. They looked at me, shrugged their shoulders, and said, "We don't mess with that." (Come again?)

Here, we had district patrols on Lake Malone, where officers from all over the district had come to saturate the lake. Many "no wake" citations were written during those efforts. Since my county had the highest number of lake houses, you can imagine whose phone rang the most with complaints after those days. The little kingdoms were certainly handling this issue differently.

Instead of citing boats for making waves, I decided not to make them myself. I did my best to drop the subject and use my best judgment.

Many people would tell me a similar story. They would say boat after boat would "wake them" all day while they fished. As soon as they started up and boated past one of those jerks who had "waked" them, at that time, a game warden would pull them over and write them a citation.

Regulating courtesy was a tricky thing, indeed.

No English

Communication with those who do not speak English is a challenge faced by many in law enforcement. Game wardens (trying to explain detailed wildlife regulations) can become very frustrated while making foreigners understand our laws. In this chapter, I'll tell how my partner and I took two different approaches to dealing with this problem on separate occasions.

On a sunny summer day, I was in a boat with my working partner and friend, Officer Tom Culton. I was driving Tom's boat on Lake Malone. We were out checking everything game wardens look for on the lake. Tom told me to steer his boat to the bridge by Shady Cliff Boat Dock. He saw a group of people fishing and planned to check their licenses.

These people were different from your typical group of fishermen. They lined up along the bank with empty soda cans in their hands. Each of those had a monofilament line wrapped around their empty can. They had a hook and bait in the water at the end of the line. While tossing their baited hooks into the lake by hand, they used the empty can as their fishing reel.

None of these men spoke English. We found out this was a group of traveling Chinese acrobats. My dear friend Tom occasionally needed help communicating with those fully versed in the English language. The foreign circus had now come to town, and my partner was in deep water over his head.

He started simply trying to communicate he was checking fishing licenses. His attempt to get his point across was going nowhere fast. Finally, the game warden stood on the boat's front, motioning and angrily yelling at the top of his lungs, "FISHING LICENSE!" to the jabbering acrobats.

While waiting for the clown car and trapeze to show up, I imagined what it would be like if he started trying to put handcuffs on this bouncing crew. Even with no mutual understanding, the argument began to get heated. For me, this was simply classic Lake Malone.

Finally, my red-faced, exasperated partner looked back at me and said two words I won't repeat. He motioned his finger, pointing down the lake, and yelled, "GO!"

I was not too fond of the thought that anyone could get away with breaking the law, no matter how primitive their fishing method was. However, this was Tom's party, and I had seen more than enough of this performance. I was ready to make the boat fly and drive away.

Not long after that day, I stopped along the Green River to check on fishermen. I was in Muhlenberg County at the Rochester Dam. Many people were fishing below the dam. One group was immediately getting nervous upon seeing me. I quickly knew these were the ones I wanted to check the most. Once again, surrounded by a group of men, they all claimed those two words, "No English."

Like my buddy Tom, I started attempting to explain I needed to see some fishing licenses. All I was getting back was shoulder shrugging and those exact two words. I was in the same predicament with this group of foreign workers that Tom had been with the Chinese acrobats. But since everyone else had to have a fishing license to fish, I was not willing to drive away.

I found a large, extended white Ford van. My big group of men (claiming they knew nothing) reluctantly nodded, admitting that was their ride. Using personally invented sign language and motioning, I let them know they were now welcome to return to fishing. I smiled and wished them a good day.

I then added one tiny key piece of information. I told the gang this van now belongs to me.

My bible tells me that a miracle took place on the day of Pentecost. It talks about a sound like a rushing mighty wind. It speaks of cloven tongues of fire appearing on their heads. I had never witnessed such events, but saw one Pentecostal miracle that day.

The biblical gift of speaking in other tongues occurred when I told them I was seizing the van. Suddenly, some started speaking English. The previous shoulder shrugging now turned into sheepish grins. Funny how that works. A wave of mutual understanding connected us while everyone fishing without a license received a citation.

I worked out a deal with a wildlife artist a few months later. We were producing the first magazine for the KY Conservation Officers. Wanting to show pictures of the different types of fish, I listed in the first magazine the size and creel limit for each fish species. I did that visually because I needed help explaining to foreigners what size and type of fish you could keep. So did everyone else if our local citizens had to abide by the laws and limits. It was that simple.

I wanted my department to use those same pictures in the yearly fishing guide. I said we were having a problem and that this would help. I was told it was not possible.

Someone in the main office devised a great idea a few years later. They would use an artist's pictures of fish in the yearly guide.

These trials were the life of a game warden. You keep slowly and painfully pushing forward, and your progress finally appears over time. Someone else may get the credit, but you know what you accomplished.

The End is Coming!

Actual court trials were usually not needed. Often, our legal prosecutions got settled ahead of time. One of the trials I attended took place in Bowling Green, Kentucky, with my working partner, Officer James Taylor.

When we got to the courthouse, I met a lovely family. These good folks had done the right thing and reported a wildlife violation. It all started one day while they were at home.

They heard a loud gunshot and looked out the window. Running through their yard, they saw an injured buck deer. Behind the deer was a man with a rifle. The man followed the buck out of the yard, where they heard another loud shot. After that, the shooter left.

They walked across their yard a few moments later and found the dead deer. The gun season was not open yet. Even if it had been in season, walking across someone else's lawn while shooting at wildlife will usually get you in trouble.

These good people knew the shooter. It was their next-door neighbor. Officer Taylor had served an arrest warrant on him for the crime. So now we were all here for the trial. In court, he was found guilty and fined accordingly.

I had thought it bizarre that someone would walk across a neighbor's lawn shooting deer, but I didn't know "bizarre" until my fellow game warden told me the rest of the story.

After these witnesses called in on the violation, they gave a written statement. An arrest warrant was issued, and game warden Jim Taylor planned to bring in his poacher.

In those days, wildlife officers drove pickup trucks with a single seat. Frequently, we would put out a radio call to a deputy sheriff or a state trooper to get help transporting those we arrested. Officer Taylor had contacted a deputy he knew to take his poacher to the jail once he got cuffs on him.

When the game warden and the deputy arrived at the poacher's house, things started going sideways. Taylor got handcuffs on his man and told him he was under arrest for poaching a deer during the closed season. After that, the show started.

While trying to get him to the deputy's car, the poacher started almost to faint one moment and then the next minute shouted, "The end is coming! Death is near! The end is coming! Death is near!"

The man who had been cool, calm, and collected while walking across a neighbor's yard shooting deer was now anything but.

The game warden finally got the ailing prophet of doom to the deputy's back seat. Just as he opened the back door to place him inside, it appeared the grim reaper came and claimed his prize. The poacher physically collapsed in the back seat, appearing to be gone.

Whenever creative actors feign passing out or death, law enforcement officers usually shake their heads and laugh or just become disgusted with the character. But no matter how fake the show may be, there is always a small percentage of doubt. So, you always take precautions to ensure they aren't dying.

I had once knocked on a man's door over an illegal trash heap. I found mail inside the dump containing his name and address. I planned to prosecute him for throwing garbage on another person's property. He saw me standing on his porch in uniform with his trash in my hand and immediately grabbed his chest and started scrambling for some Nitroglycerin tablets. Of course, I immediately started wondering if this was an act to get out of a citation or if my presence could cause a heart attack. I got that one calmed down and later served him a summons for the illegal dumping.

Officer Taylor stood by the deputy sheriff's car with his poacher appearing dead in the back seat. The game warden and the deputy looked at each other, shaking their heads. Still, Taylor was keeping one eye on the guy just in case.

I have read that even after death, the body makes specific movements. That's due to contractions in muscles. When a few muscles contract at the same time, it twitches. It appeared this same thing was happening with our dead poacher. Taylor watched as one part of him started moving.

In those days, many deputies drove a large sedan with a cage in the back seat. Their rear seating area consisted of bars with a screen or shield. Two things got removed back there. Those were the door handles. The back doors only opened from the outside. Empty holes were the only things located inside where the handles used to be.

As the game warden kept one eye peeled on that back seat, one part of the poacher's dead body slowly started to move. Those after-death twitches must have settled into one of his hands.

Even though his body was stone-cold dead, the fingers of that one hand were feeling around the empty hole in the back door of the deputy's car. It appeared the dead hand was searching for something that was not there.

The tiny movements brought a chuckle to the game warden and the deputy. They no longer needed to worry in the least about their dead passenger. They now knew he would be resurrected entirely as soon as they got him to the jail.

Temper Temper

Game wardens try not to let frustrations get the best of them. Most stay professional even under trying circumstances. But occasionally, things happen, and tempers flare. In this chapter, I'll share a few of those times.

My friend Tom Culton was the game warden in Muhlenberg County. Tom could be professional when needed, but his temper caused him to color outside the lines a few times.

One day, Tom was patrolling Lake Malone when he got into a shouting match with an older gentleman at the lake's dam. The man had yelled at Tom's boat. He was angry about all the trash along the dam. He wanted to tell the officer what he should do about this garbage.

Things quickly got heated as they yelled back and forth at each other. Finally, the angry man wanted to know the officer's name so he could call the Frankfort office and report him. My dear buddy Tom yelled back at him, "My name is Jeff Finn!" and then sped off in his boat.

Later that day, I came motoring down the lake in my boat. A grinning Tom met me and said, "You probably don't want to get around the dam today." He then laughed and told me why. I thanked him for throwing me under the bus and immediately started plotting my next practical joke on him. At least my friend was always good for a laugh on Lake Malone.

One time, tempers flared, and no one was laughing. Tom was in a boat patrolling Lake Malone with Eddie Young. Eddie was the game warden in Hopkins County. Tom was driving the boat on a hot weekend with wall-to-wall people on the lake. According to our regulations, swimming in the lake was only allowed at the designated beach area.

It is difficult to explain what it's like trying to make everyone stay out of the water on a hot, crowded day at the lake. It's like herding cats.

There was one rowdy group at the state park. They were jumping off the large rocks and swimming. The two game wardens in their boat pulled up to that crowd in the water. Officer Young started explaining the lake regulations concerning swimming. He told them they must drive to the beach to get in the water.

Of course, this group had already consumed some beer, so after making a few snarky remarks, they all crawled out of the water and just sat there dripping on the rocks, staring at the game wardens. It didn't appear anyone was driving to the beach. The two hot and sweating game wardens motored off in their boat, knowing this was not over.

After one more patrol around the lake, the two officers returned to the state park to see the whole crowd again in the water. A few more of those hidden beers had been consumed. Tempers flared as they were again ordered to get out of the water. The angry mob continued mouthing off to the game wardens.

Officer Young was now standing in the boat, expounding what would occur if they failed to comply with the law. My buddy Tom had gotten quiet. He was now silent but hot in more ways than one.

As Eddie was telling them what to do, Tom idled the boat around to face away from the fuming bunch. Eddie noticed the boat motor tilt upward as Tom hit the trim button. Just when the prop neared the top of the water, my angry buddy allowed his temper to win out. He jammed the throttle forward, causing a huge rooster tail of water to hose down the angry mob. Evidently, Tom thought if they wanted to get wet, he would help them out.

This maneuver certainly did not cool them off. It did just the opposite. Somehow, after lots of shouting, things finally settled without bloodshed. After hearing that story, I always asked people to stay close to the bank if they got in the water to cool off so a passing boat would not hit them. It was not the perfect solution, but perfection was always hard to find at Lake Malone.

On another occasion, I witnessed an impressive shouting match. My friend Tom and I were out checking spring turkey hunting. Tom had gotten a complaint about some illegal hunting. We drove back to an old dead-end road, where we encountered a hunter. It was our subject.

Officer Culton approached him and started checking him. The game warden told him that he was in violation. Our turkey poacher immediately flew mad and started yelling. I felt like Tom would soon arrest this guy, but he didn't. Instead, he started yelling right back at him.

I just stood there watching the heated shouting match for some time. When the two men finally stopped to catch their breath, I calmly asked them, "Are you both through?". The poacher said nothing while Tom apologized to me for letting this guy get under his skin.

After that, I started writing the man his citation. I never thought I would run into that guy again, but one day I did.

One of my local farmers called me about a hunter trespassing on his land. I met with the farmer, and he told me about their confrontation. He identified the man. It was the same man with whom Tom got into the shouting match.

I told the landowner that if he gave me a written statement, I would get charges filed for hunting without permission. He gave me the write-up, and I went and got a criminal summons from my county attorney.

There is a massive factory in my assigned county. Many people work there, and I knew my trespasser was one of those. Once I got my criminal summons, I called the factory's main office to see if this man was at work. I identified myself, telling them I was a state law enforcement officer with a summons I needed to serve. They told me he was at work. I thanked them and told them I'd be down there immediately to serve this summons.

At what seemed like lightning speed, my phone rang. It was my trespasser. He begged me to meet him at the convenience store after work. I agreed to do that. It felt good that I would not have to hunt high and low for my subject this time.

When we both arrived at the store, he was upset and a little flabbergasted that I would consider coming to his large factory to serve him a criminal summons. He wanted to know how I could embarrass him before his bosses and coworkers.

First off, I let him know it was not me who would have embarrassed him. I told him he had done this to himself when he hunted on a farm without permission. Secondly, I reminded him that I had watched him shouting at the top of his lungs in the face of a game warden. I told him I wasn't about to head to some unknown dead-end road to find his house and possibly a group of angry relatives.

I let him know for officer safety purposes, I would be serving any future summons at his workplace. If he didn't want to get embarrassed in front of his bosses, he probably needed to only hunt on land where he had permission.

Fortunately, I never dealt with him a single time after that. Years later, I learned he and Officer Tom Culton had somehow become friends. I didn't see that one coming. Life was always full of surprises.

On another occasion, I was patrolling in Warren County, Kentucky, with Officer Jim Taylor. It was springtime, and we were out checking fishermen. As we headed down one road, we saw someone fishing at a small lake. There was a house located beside it. A tiny walkway bridge ran from the house over to the water.

Jim quickly turned around before the person fishing could see us. I wanted to understand why we were stopping. Once he got his truck hidden, he started explaining something to me.

This attempt was not the first time the game warden had tried to check people fishing at this lake. On previous occasions, as soon as they saw an official vehicle, everyone would run across that walkway bridge and then hide in the house. Today, Taylor had the plan to put a stop to this game.

Jim told me to drive and to let him out in the woods near the house. He would ease up through the woods and get close to the home. At that time, I was to drive to the far side of the lake to check the person fishing. If he took off running this time, he would get a surprise on that walkway bridge.

So, we put his plan into motion. He started creeping up through the woods. I gave him plenty of time to get set up and ready. Then I started our game warden truck and drove down the road. When reaching the far side of the lake, I turned off the road and started driving up a field road to the water. When my fisherman saw me coming, he grabbed everything and took off running just like Taylor said he would.

It was the first time I had ever watched someone running away from me while I sat still with a big smile on my face, watching the show. The runner was making great time heading straight toward that house. As he started to zip across that walkway bridge, he looked up to see a large, tall, smiling game warden blocking his escape route. The jig was up.

The person fishing was from somewhere other than this area. They did not have a fishing license. I got turned around in the truck and drove over to assist.

As we prepared to write him a citation, a furious young man came storming out of the house, running his mouth. Taylor told him their little game of hide and seek was over. Until this point, only one person was losing his temper, but that almost changed after the following words shot out.

When he finally saw they were busted, the seething guy looked straight at Officer James Taylor and hissed, "You won't always be wearing that badge."

I looked at my partner's eyes as they narrowed like a laser beam. The running mouth had been looking for a nerve to strike, and with that line, he found it.

The big game warden took one step closer to him, looked him dead in the eyes, and said, "You're (bleep) right, and I'll take it off right now if you want me to."

For a few seconds, we had ourselves a little moment there. I quickly looked for my baton in case the fan was about to be hit with that stinky stuff. But our little mouthy buddy blinked. He decided he did not want that badge to come off after all. He made a wise choice.

Since I've talked about a few times when my fellow officers almost lost their cool, it would only be fair to tell on myself. I have never been comfortable showing my temper, so hardly ever did I lose it. Although one time I did, and of all things, it was over a boat dock.

My department regulated the personal boat docks on Lake Malone. The older officers worked on those laws and the property issues around the lake for years. When enforcing any regulation, you can handle things in a few different ways.

When a state trooper enforces speeding, he must decide the magic number before a citation is written. If the speed limit is 55, most KY troopers allow you a grace area of a few MPH. Whenever I drive through Ohio, that grace area decreases.

Before I became one of the game wardens on Lake Malone, the older officers had not cited anyone with a boat dock that was a foot or two over the regulation. To them, it was like someone driving 57 MPH in a 55-speed zone. They similarly handled property issues on the department's fifty feet of ground around the lake.

Many small things have happened throughout the years. The department once attempted to stop grass mowing on their property. A public outcry caused that to fail. Eventually, the enforcement of all regulations concerning those living around the water grew lax.

Then, one day, I knocked over the first domino in a long line of dominos that extended around the entire state of Kentucky.

Sometimes, when you want to be a low-key person, someone takes a hand on your back and pushes you into the spotlight. I had been following the lead of the officers before me. Up till this point, I had just kept a lid on things. Then my phone started ringing as that lid got ready to blow.

I received several phone calls that someone had built a new boat dock on Lake Malone. All the callers were saying the same thing. This dock was huge. They claimed it was way bigger than everyone else's. What made it even worse was that it sat inside the ski channel on a corner of the bend in the lake. The placement could be a danger to someone skiing around that corner. They could run into this oversized dock and be injured or killed. This driver was not someone doing 57 MPH in a 55 zone. This bandit was flying past me at 90.

I drove to the lake and saw the problem. All the callers were correct. I found out the carpenter's name was who built this dock. I was well aware of him. He also had a lake house and dock just a few doors down. He had made many docks and knew all about their regulated size restrictions. He would laugh at those regulations and build you any size dock you wanted if he made his money.

I knew this one had gone too far. This dock's size was not a minor violation. I contacted the owner and prepared to issue him a citation for an illegal structure. I wanted them to change the size of it to make it legal and no longer a hazard to anyone on the lake.

I traveled to the owner's office to issue this citation. He had flown somewhere on business. He had a male secretary who told me I could leave the ticket with him. Sitting in a plush office and handing a citation to a secretary seemed quite different from sitting on a log while citing a coonhunter. It was all very polite, and I knew attorneys would handle it from that point forward.

During court proceedings, their attorney brought up the many minor violations around the lake. He felt it unfair to cite his client and not cite them all, and the judge agreed. So now my department has a decision to make. If we wanted to stop this guy driving 90 MPH, we would have to cite everyone driving 56 MPH.

Some may not agree with this analogy. I do know quite a few dock owners who do agree. (They shared feelings quite freely while I wrote their citations.)

While standing in the eye of this hurricane and watching all the debris circling me, I couldn't help but think about the laughing carpenter who lit the fuse and built the colossal dock. Our laws and regulations list that anyone who facilitates or makes money from a violation is equally guilty. This man knew full well the legal size of a boat dock, and I wanted him to stop making money off illegal ones.

With this last dock, he had caused problems for many people. (Or had made many to comply with the law, depending on how you looked at this all.) Either way, he was the one person walking away laughing with a pocket full of money, and I wanted some words.

So, the day I lost my cool was in the middle of the crowded Shady Cliff Boat Dock Restaurant at lunchtime, where I found my laughing carpenter. I did not plan for it to happen. I wanted this man to tell me he would quit building oversized docks. But the more I explained the problems he was causing, the more he snickered and claimed none of this mattered.

As he ate lunch, I stood beside his table and explained that he could be charged for making money from these violations. The more I talked, the more he made fun of everything I was trying to tell him. It was all a big joke to him.

I really don't get mad, but this man was making my temperature rise more with every dismissive laughing word he said. The marina owner's son was standing there watching all this. He could see the red as it pushed up into my face. Just before I opened my mouth again, he grabbed the builder and pulled him aside.

I could hear him whispering to the man. He said, "I've known that game warden a long time, and I've never seen him mad. But you have made him hot, and he is fixing to arrest you and take you to jail if you don't shut up." He knew the early warning signs of a trip to jail and was not wrong.

Finally, the man quit laughing and got quiet. I admit I was red-faced, and my hand shook when I told him to hand me his driver's license. I went outside and wrote him a citation for illegal facilitation, returned to the restaurant, and gave it to him. No more words were said. I'm sorry for the other patrons who got dinner and a show that day.

After all this, my department started monitoring boat dock issues more closely and developed a new system to keep records. I learned a few lessons myself. I returned to keeping a cool head and a calm demeanor when dealing with violators.

FROM THE GAME WARDEN'S CAMPFIRE

Enjoying a Day Off

Getting to enjoy a day off for a game warden can be difficult. A relaxing time is tough if you plan to go hunting or fishing. You may work five days in a row without running into any violations. If you take a day off, one always pops up in your face. Don't even think about trying to go duck hunting.

I can't remember all the times it happened to me. It felt like it was never-ending. I remember deciding to take a day off and go fishing. It was a pretty spring day, and I planned to take my whole family along.

Usually, I preferred wading in small, secluded streams when fishing. But on this day, since I was taking everyone along, I thought we needed some extra elbow room. I opted to take them to the spillway of Barren River Lake.

I worked in the spillway area a lot, checking fishing. We often did stakeouts there for those illegally snagging below the dam. Since I wanted to be utterly off-work today, I walked my family a reasonable distance below the dam. I got us set up in an area facing away from the dam. I didn't even want to be able to see if someone started snagging. I didn't want anything to distract me from this day of family fishing fun. (You already see this coming, don't you?)

I fixed us up near the campground, hoping we might catch some crappie or white bass. Soon, I discovered that you must also bring earplugs no matter which direction you face or how good your visual blinders are.

A guy fishing at the river's bend starts shouting to everyone around us. He yells at the top of his lungs, "I've caught a big rainbow trout, and I don't have a trout stamp! Who wants this trout?"

I look around to see him standing there with a big trout while yelling the same thing repeatedly. There was a reason why I liked fishing in secluded streams like my father. It could happen even there, but usually, in those places, I could enjoy a day of fishing without having to stop and write a citation.

At times, funny things could happen, too. Once, I was in Muhlenberg County with a friend. We stopped by the house of some relatives. The husband at this house was a bird hunter. He had bird dogs and hunted quail. I also had a small pointer bird dog and hunted quail then. The man's wife did not know who I was or that I was a game warden. Her husband, however, did know.

Before anyone introduced me, the wife discovered I had a bird dog. At that, the lady of the house came alive! She was a real talker. She quickly started telling me about her husband having bird dogs, too. Then she said how many quail he had already killed that morning and over the last few days. She was hardly taking a breath as the numbers were starting to pile up.

I looked over at her husband and cracked a small smile. He, on the other hand, was not smiling at all. His face was turning a bright shade of red, and he was getting madder and madder the more his wife counted dead quail numbers in front of the game warden.

Finally, she stopped to catch her breath. My friend decided it was time to introduce me, saying, "You may not know him, but this is Jeff Finn. He's a game warden." A look of panic swept across the poor lady's face.

Then, the chatty woman's husband decided it was his turn to speak. He glared at his wife and spat these words at her, "Now, why don't you run your (Bleep) mouth some more!"

I felt sorry for the poor gal, even though I couldn't help but laugh. Introductions should always come first when it comes to game wardens.

I was Wrong

No one is perfect. Occasionally, game wardens misunderstand things. We don't see what we think we see, or we look for one thing but find something entirely different. Here are a few of the times that happened to me.

In Simpson County, KY, the locals call one deserted stretch of road "Spray Paint Road." They gave it that handle after many young people started practicing their artistic talents on it using cans of spray paint. Kids like deserted roads for their own reasons, while game wardens like them for something different. Years ago, I occasionally did a nighttime stakeout on that road for illegal hunting.

There was a grown-up area just off that road. I could go far into the bushes and hide my patrol truck. No houses were anywhere close to me. It looked like the perfect spot to catch some illegal night hunters. Game wardens do these kinds of stakeouts for hours, waiting to see if someone comes to kill wildlife illegally. Occasionally, it's not poachers who show up.

On this night, I had gotten off the road and had hidden my marked truck well. Hours passed while nothing happened. Occasionally, a car might drive down the colorful painted pavement without stopping or doing anything else. It was a typical boring night until that all stopped.

It was reasonably late, and I watched a car slowly drive along the road. This one did not move on through. It stopped and started backing into the same brushy field road where I was. It was a sharp-looking little Ford Mustang.

It appeared they wanted to hide, just like I did. Their only problem was that they didn't come back into the bushes as far as my truck. So, they never noticed the game warden's vehicle parked behind them. (They probably had other things on their mind.)

I quickly realized the clean Mustang was not full of coonhunters or spotlighters. No lights came on when I stepped outside of my truck due to some specialty covert wiring. I grabbed my mag light and eased out to approach the car in the dark. I knew if a truckload of poachers came down the road now, I wouldn't be able to give chase. This hot sports car had blocked my vehicle's path.

When I neared the car, I saw a teenage boy and a girl inside it. They should consider themselves lucky that I didn't wait long to approach them. (Just saying)

Some activity had already started in the first few moments. A small light shone inside the vehicle. I could see the young man was busy. He had a white piece of paper in his hand. The driver seemed to be rolling something. This case was not turning into much of a mystery.

Soon, a lighter spit out a tiny flame. Both occupants took a hit from the newly formed joint as I turned on my mag light and tapped on the driver's window. (Talk about a buzz kill.)

At times, things happen fast. At other times, things happen flying squirrel fast. Flying squirrel fast is a whole lot faster. After seeing a flashlight, badge, and gun, stuff started moving inside the Mustang, resembling those nocturnal rodent speedsters. Their eyes were big like them, too.

I got them both out, and we had our little "Come to Jesus" moment. I wonder if the Mustang ever backed into another hiding spot without looking hard first for a hidden game warden.

On another evening, I was doing a late-night poaching patrol in Logan County. A good couple I knew and liked were having some poaching problems. They oversaw a lot of acres on a massive farm and a few huge bucks fed in the fields. Those sightings draw in poachers like magnets. The couple hoped I could help them in some way to stop the illegal activity on these grounds.

The gravel drive going back to their house seemed to go forever. Poachers could get on this road without the homeowners knowing they were out there. The outlaws only needed to turn around before reaching the couple's home at the far end.

I drove out to the farm and got on this gravel road. I found an old barn where I could hide my truck behind. I then settled in for a long night of nothing. But tonight, nothing turned into something.

It was late, and I hadn't seen a soul. I thought about just leaving. Then, from out of nowhere, I was seeing headlights coming into my road. They were driving slowly. This vehicle was a game changer, making things look promising.

They came past me and then kept easing on down the road slowly. I could watch them for a long way. I was expecting to see the spotlight come out at any time. It never did.

After getting far up the road, this vehicle stopped and turned out its lights. At that point, I changed gears and thought I would soon hear raccoon dogs. They had to be a group of coonhunters.

No dogs ever started barking, so I wasn't sure what was happening with this vehicle. It was time for me to get a closer look.

I flipped the switch that killed all the lights on my truck. The distance between me and this vehicle made me want to drive instead of walk. I could picture myself walking halfway up there, and then it takes off, flying by me, with me having no way to stop it. So, I started my slow drive in the dark as I approached my target.

Gravel makes that popping noise when an automobile moves on top of it. On this night, I didn't realize how much noise my truck made in those rocks. Before reaching the point where I planned to stop and hide, tires started spinning in the gravel as the vehicle I was watching shot out of its hiding place!

I planned to block them since this was a long, dead-end road. There was one tiny problem with my plan. They weren't coming towards me. They were heading back towards the landowner's house and speeding to get there.

I wasn't sure if I was now running poachers, drug addicts, or thieves straight to this couple's house in the middle of the night. I knew whatever was happening, I needed to check on this fast.

As I made it to the dark house at the end of the drive, a teenage girl was darting inside it. A car sat there in front of me with its motor running. With the mystery now solved, I hated to turn around and leave without explaining something to the parents. It turned out no explanation was necessary.

In a few moments, the front door of the house opened. A mother in her housecoat came walking out to my truck. She was looking right at me with an odd little smile. A wise mom said, "Jeff, there's no need to say anything. You probably saved me more than a poached deer tonight, and I thank you."

I smiled and nodded. At that time, I left so a mother could have one of those heart-to-heart talks with the young man sitting in that car.

One bright sunny day, I felt confident I was seeing one thing, which turned out to be something else. I was checking fishing licenses at the city park in Bowling Green, KY. They have a good-sized lake, and I had stopped to check everything out.

My truck sat hidden in a parking lot among some other vehicles. I was sitting in it using my binoculars to scan the lake. No one was fishing on the far side of the water. There were, however, many people over there watching a kid's ballgame. It looked like a typical day for families to get out and have fun.

I saw one man leave the bleachers and come to the lake. He didn't have fishing tackle, so I initially felt like there was nothing to see here. Then, as he approached the water, he dropped down over the bank's edge and got into a hiding position. He was looking around to make sure no one could see him. No one could see him except for a hidden game warden with binoculars.

Now, this guy had my full attention. He got to messing with something in his pocket, and soon, he was lighting something and smoking it, all the time staying low and hidden. Occasionally, he would ease his head high enough to ensure no one could see him from the bleachers.

At the time, I had little doubt. I felt sure the man was at a city park ballgame with his kids, and I saw him taking a break to smoke pot. Our department was working hard to make public fishing areas drug-free zones. I planned to drive around and have a conversation with this guy.

I watched while he finished his joint. He stepped on it, mashing it into the ground, and then returned to the bleachers. With my binoculars, I could still see the tiny white spot that I felt was the marijuana roach that he stamped out. I marked its location in my mind using the rocks and trees around it as markers. Then, I started my patrol vehicle and headed to a ball game.

The blue lights were not flashing, but the marked truck got folks' attention anyway as heads snapped in my direction. I pulled up to the bleachers and stepped out in uniform, walking straight to the man I had been watching. I asked him if he would come with me for a moment. His wife seemed quite nervous. I tried calming her by saying I only needed a few minutes of his time. My attempt at easing fears did not work.

I got the man to start walking back with me to my evidence. He immediately wanted to know what this was all about. I told him, "This is about you being unable to watch a kids' ballgame without smoking a joint behind the bleachers."

He quickly blurted out, "I never smoked a joint!" I responded, "We both know that's a lie because I just watched you do it."

By this time, we had reached the water's edge. I looked down at my memorized markers. There lay the tiny white spot of evidence. It was a Marlboro Light cigarette butt.

I looked at him, confused. He hung his head and said, "I've been lying to my wife and kids that I've quit smoking, but I'm pretty sure you have brought that all to a stop today."

I apologized for my mistake and am sure more apologies and explanations occurred afterward.

One night, I partnered up with the McLean County game warden. Officer Frankie Cox and I were working on a district air patrol. Officers were paired up from all over the district as a couple of game wardens worked as spotters from an airplane.

On this night, we patrolled the northern counties of our area. Each pair of officers had been assigned to a stakeout location while they waited to see if the plane found any poachers in their area.

The terrain in our assigned spot differed significantly from the southern counties where I usually worked. It had small rolling hills but was wide open. You could see for miles.

This night's leader said there was a barn we could hide behind in our area. I hoped that was true because if it weren't, a poacher's spotlight would be able to shine and light up my truck from a mile away.

We drove down a long, dead-end field road for quite a while. Finally, I came upon the barn where I could hide my truck. We settled in for a long night. At least the plane was flying so we won't get bored.

The airplane did not give us a single call that night. A few other game wardens caught some poachers while we hung out behind our barn in the middle of nowhere. But before the night was over, I finally saw headlights, and they were coming our way.

There was nothing in this entire country but this one barn, not even a tree, so I felt sure the spotlight would be coming out soon. It never did.

From miles away, I watched those headlights approaching us. I was playing a cat-and-mouse game with my truck, slowly moving it with minor adjustments to stay behind the only thing I had to hide behind: my barn.

There was no way these were coonhunters. There was not a tree for a raccoon to climb in this country. Finally, the vehicle made its way back to our barn.

I stationed my truck on one side of this barn. The newcomers parked on the opposite end. Since they were not the farmers coming to check on their equipment and weren't poachers, the list of what they might be doing in the middle of the night was narrowing down.

Since I may need to stop this vehicle, I stayed behind the wheel. Officer Cox eased out in the dark to see what brought them back here. A few minutes later, he returned and said, "Well, they ain't hunting or fishing."

If you plan to hide in the middle of nowhere, just realize you may not be the only one hiding.

During my first few years as a game warden, the Simpson County school system merged all their grade schools. This consolidation meant several county elementary school buildings would get auctioned off to buyers. My mom was not afraid to purchase something if she felt it was a good buy. So, my mother attended the auction and purchased the Barnes Elementary School property, where I had spent my first six years of learning as a young boy.

There were two large buildings at this old school property. A brick building sat in the front. It had been the primary school. An older stone building in the back had served as a gym and cafeteria. It also had a couple of older classrooms attached.

My family had worked on these two buildings. We made a livable apartment in the brick building. The old gym got turned into a small side business where guys paid to come out and play basketball. On the side, a game room with pool tables, pinball machines, and video games entertained those not shooting hoops.

My mother also purchased some old vending machines. She would go to the discount "Day Old Bakery" and fill her machines with treats and snacks. Of course, she had cold drink machines she kept filled also. It quickly turned into a nighttime hangout. Business always picked up as soon as the tobacco stripping season had ended.

Even though this was a home with a business, it still appeared to be a vacant schoolhouse. My father would get frustrated with the "riffraff" that would show up.

A guy with a metal detector showed up one day. Without asking permission, he started going around digging holes in our property. When we told him it was private property, he became rude. Dad claimed he would fill his rear end with birdshot and ask if he could "detect" that.

After becoming a game warden, I started getting accustomed to dealing with some of the ones who frustrated my dad. I tried to keep a watch on things. One night, I almost saw too much.

I was parked out back behind the old school building. It was late at night. I heard a vehicle easing onto the property. I thought I was about to catch some vandals or thieves.

At the far end of the front building, we had an exterior light that stayed on. It was directly below an extensive set of concrete steps. It was our tiny way of saying this place belongs to someone. I knew the car had stopped not far from that end. I grabbed my light and started around the back of the building to see who was out there.

As I rounded the back corner of the building, I could see a vehicle idling in the front with its parking lights on. I took a few more steps and saw something under our light on the side of the building. The concrete steps were partially blocking my view. I could only see the top of whatever it was that I was seeing.

I finally decided I was seeing a small child standing underneath our light. I wondered why a young kid would be standing there late at night. I turned on my light and stepped forward, intending to say, "Honey, can I help you?" I only got out the first word.

I had now stepped past those concrete steps that blocked my view. It turned out I was not seeing the head of a young child. Instead, I looked at a grown woman squatting down, relieving herself under my porch light.

When I spoke that first word, "honey," an ear-piercing scream filled the air! The cry continued while she was trying to run and get clothed simultaneously. She somehow dived into the car's passenger side as it sped off. I then searched for a garden hose to wash off a long section of my sidewalk. It seemed like game wardens ran into stuff even at home.

FROM THE GAME WARDEN'S CAMPFIRE

Two Things I Disliked

Two things that came along with the game warden job that I didn't particularly care for were working baited areas for wild turkey poachers and walking where you couldn't see venomous snakes. Both of those two things gave me some pause. I have a couple of stories about both topics.

Some officers loved working turkey bait. I had no misgivings about waterfowl bait, but I didn't enjoy the turkey stakeouts for a reason. When working duck or dove bait, you didn't have to sit right on top of it. At least with them, my poachers could see me coming and know I was a person.

The part of turkey bait that bothered me was moving in the woods beside someone ready to shoot fast at a bird. I was okay whenever I could get them to see I was not a wild turkey.

Any poacher could take a shot at a game warden. I prepared for that. Angry outlaws never bothered me as much as overly excited shooters did. You could also add those who shoot at low birds on a dove field to the list.

Walking in venomous snake country kept me alert, especially after dark with no light. When I transferred from Simpson County to Logan County, I left an area with very few copperheads and almost no rattlesnakes to one with plenty of both and a small portion of cottonmouth water moccasins in the swampy areas of its northern section. That made running after coonhunters in the dark quite interesting.

The cottonmouth population was small, and I only walked a small amount in the swamps where they made their home. The timber rattlesnakes were honorable enough to give you a warning and attempted to get away from you. The more plentiful copperheads did neither.

I had worked with Logan County's previous conservation officer for three years before transferring to his county when he retired. Officer Joe Pillow had given me some warnings about snakes. He told me about a day he checked fishing licenses with Gerald Barnett, the game warden in Todd County. They were walking around a watershed lake in northern Todd County. Joe said as he started to put one foot down, he looked, and it was about to go down right on top of a coiled-up copperhead. I asked Joe what he did. He replied, "I took one giant step and kept stepping fast!"

When the two game wardens returned, a local bootlegger looked at the copperhead. He told the two officers he could snap the snake and pop its neck to kill it. So, the bootlegger snapped it, saying it was now dead.

He put it in a jar and gave it to Joe. Barnett drove Officer Pillow back to his truck at Shady Cliff Boat Dock. When they got out of the vehicle, a very much live copperhead repeatedly struck the glass in the jar. The bootlegger obviously needed to improve his snake-killing technique.

I often thought about Joe almost stepping on that copperhead while easing around the watershed lakes. But then Gerald Barnett had something happen that topped Joe's ordeal.

Not far from my new home was a watershed lake. When I first moved here, it was odd that almost everyone I checked fishing at that lake was from my old home county. It appeared word had gotten out about it having some good bluegill. So many older men I considered my regulars would often be fishing there. Most carried some form of protection for snakes. There was a good reason why.

One day, Gerald Barnett headed to that lake to check fishing. You had to squeeze through some large boulders to make your way down. While easing between the big rocks, he felt a pop to the side of his leg. Joe's story had just gotten beat, however, like they say in the commercials, "But wait! There's more!"

Officer Barnett had always been a big believer in snake boots. He wore knee-high protection in case of an incident like the one that just happened. At times, he wore these on the outside of his pants legs, but today, he had pulled his green game warden jeans down over the top of his boots. That was about to play a keen role in what happened next.

When Gerald felt the pop, he looked down to see a nice fat copperhead. This one wasn't lying on the ground. It was firmly attached to his green jeans.

When the snake hit, his protective boots kept it from getting the venom in his leg, but its fangs had become tangled in the denim of his jeans. The twisting copperhead now couldn't pull itself loose. That's what you call a problem.

If you've ever been to a Celtic celebration, you may have seen some of the traditional Irish dancers. They make an impressive, lively dance move, bouncing on one foot while kicking with the other.

For a few seconds, Barnett did an accelerated version of that dance. One foot was hopping while the other was stomping, trying to knock the venomous fangs of the copperhead loose from the game warden's britches. It would have made any leprechaun proud.

Finally, he freed himself from the viper, pulled out his service weapon, and laid it to rest. After hearing that story, it had me shopping for snake boots.

The turkey bait stakeouts got game wardens up early. You had to beat the shooter to his spot and then watch and see if he hunts there. You also must go there beforehand to document the bait as evidence. I'm glad trail cameras weren't out yet when I did it.

Gerald Barnett contacted me once to work turkey bait with him. He had found out about some and had already been there to document it. He had run into a snag when he went there to collect his evidence.

The two men who were going to be hunting there had seen him. They were not from Barnett's county, so they didn't know he was the game warden. He had slipped in to take pictures of the wheat seeds while wearing camo clothing.

The two guys got angry and confronted him, wanting to know what he was doing in there. He told them he had just gotten lost by mistake. He apologized and told them he would leave. They weren't happy about it, but they told him just to be sure and stay off the property. The next day was the opening day of the spring wild turkey season, and their trespasser and I were heading right back in there again.

On opening morning, we got out of bed about two hours before the turkey hunters did and then headed to our baited area. We had to go the long way in from the backside. (as usual) We found our spot and then got hidden under some camouflage netting. It was time to sit in the dark and wait for poachers. After a while, we heard a motor running. Our prom dates were making their way to us.

When I saw their flashlights start through the woods, I soon realized they would be walking beside us. We stayed still under the camo net as they approached. Their lights seemed to bounce off everything around us. Just as they passed within inches of me, I got a whiff of something. Our two poachers had a shotgun in one hand and were smoking a joint with the other. (How lovely.) At least maybe these two won't be hyper and shooting fast.

We let them set up in the baited area, and they began to sound off using turkey calls. We talked about how long to wait but knew we had seen enough. There was no need to let these two kill any wildlife today.

Barnett stood up first to approach them. We were still in camo clothing at this point. Our two guys look to see the trespasser who they ran off yesterday. They were mad at him then. Today, they are furious at his return.

Their trespasser, however, is just standing there smiling at them. Just before their temperature pops a cork, I stand up, and Barnett pulls out a big shiny badge. (Total buzz kill)

When you realize your trespasser was the game warden and you had already met him yesterday, yet you still came and hunted in an illegally baited area, what else can you say?

Maybe they were high yesterday, too. (I think they should go with that one.)

We disarmed our poachers, and I started to write their citations. One of the two poachers began acting strange. I should say, stranger.

For some reason, he decides he will try and pick up the shotgun we have taken away from him. While I'm writing tickets, I hear Barnett loudly say, "If you try to touch that gun, we're fixing to have some real problems here! You better back up and stay away from it!"

I pause my citation writing long enough to see if I need my ink pen or my 45 in my hand. We all have a little moment.

After that, our poachers start making better decisions. There was rarely a dull moment on the opening day of turkey season.

Joe Pillow and Tom Caudill

Ever since the 5th grade at Barnes Elementary School, I had wanted to be a game warden. In those days, Conservation Officer Tom Caudill would come and speak to our class and show us films. My father believed the man was one of the most honest and fair men anywhere. If my dad respected him, that meant something. I hoped to one day wear the same uniform as Officer Caudill.

When I became old enough, I started taking the state merit exam. While attempting to fulfill my dream, I finally got called in for several interviews. One was for a wildlife officer job in Breathitt County; another was for Edmonson. I didn't get hired. Jamon Halvaksz got Breathitt while Sammie Renfro snatched Edmonson. I wasn't giving up, though.

On your state job application, you could list a second option. If you couldn't get the one you wanted, you might still get employed. I listed Park Ranger as my second choice. It wasn't my dream job, but would be an excellent way to get my foot in the door.

One day, I got a call from the manager at the Columbus-Belmont State Park. He needed a park ranger and wanted to interview me. John S. Adams said I needed to get to the park fast if I wanted this job. He claimed there was a problem with my politics.

In those days, a political contact person from the governor's office had to approve all new hires. You only got hired if you registered with the same political party as him. The park superintendent said I signed up with the wrong side.

But he also said the political contact guy was on vacation. So, if I could get there fast, he could sneak around and get me hired before the guy returned home.

After a quick trip to the furthest point west in Kentucky, I became the only ranger for a tiny scenic park hanging off a bluff above the Mississippi River. I patrolled the walkways at night, watching barges and riverboats travel up and down the river. On Sunday afternoons, I tried to catch teenagers speeding and drinking beer. One year passed, and I kept wanting to be a game warden.

After working there for several months, I learned that Officer Tom Caudill, who had inspired me, was retiring. More than anything, I wanted his slot and to move back home. I drove to my former game warden's house on my day off. I asked him if he had any tips for me to get hired. He had a suggestion. It made me cringe.

Tom and his wife Edith invited me into their lovely home. They were good, fine people. When I asked him what I needed to do, he said, "The way I can help you the most is for you to pretend like you don't know me." (Say what?)

My mentor and idol went on to say he and his partner and friend Joe Pillow had both had a falling out with the boss who would be doing the hiring for the position. If I wanted my dream job, I would have to pretend I didn't know (or even like) the two men whom I would come to respect the most.

If there is one thing I have excelled at in life, it is my ability to ignore red flags. I always had that one down pat. I sat in Tom Caudill's living room while he waved a big red flag (possibly several), and I still wanted that job anyway.

So, I left the home of the man my dad highly respected and started pretending I didn't know or like him. (The things we do.)

Tom Caudill's advice did help me to get hired. Soon, I was moving back home to become a game warden.

During my first three years on the job, while assigned to Simpson County, I bordered three other counties. Each of those three had a different officer. My boss tried to ensure I only worked with two of those three officers. He wanted me to work with anyone other than Joe Pillow in Logan County.

Joe Pillow was one of the most honorable men I knew. He was a fine officer who was well respected in his county. Any time I could pull some strings to where I could work with Joe, I would jump at the chance to do so. I learned a lot from his wise outlook on the job.

When he retired, I transferred and took over his county. He was always a wealth of information for me. I loved sitting and hearing the game warden stories Joe would tell of years gone by. There was one that always amazed me.

Doing nighttime stakeouts to catch poachers spotlighting deer was always a big thing for game wardens. We all did that a lot. It was always more exciting when the airplane was flying and doing the spotting for us. You had an excellent chance to catch someone on those nights.

The nights that you worked alone without the plane could be boring. On those nights, you often caught no one. Occasionally, after weeks of nothing, you would finally bust some bad guys.

The older officers, like Joe, had worked back in the day when a lot more wildlife crime took place. Those guys could thrill you with stories of chasing poachers or getting after different ones using dip nets to seine fish in the creeks and rivers. Joe had this one story that I thought about a lot during those lonely nighttime stakeouts.

Coopertown Road is a rural stretch of highway running up in northern Logan County. Years ago, Officers Joe Pillow and Tom Caudill were doing a nighttime stakeout for deer poachers on this road. The airplane was not flying on this night. It was just two game wardens hiding their truck while sitting and waiting to see if any spotlighters came through trying to kill a deer. Tonight, luck was on their side.

During this time, officers were driving their personal vehicles. There were no marked state vehicles back then. Joe said a truck came down the road, shining a spotlight shortly after he got his pickup hidden in a remote field.

Back then, game wardens had an old blue light they could hold in their hand. It plugged into your cigarette lighter. They plugged in their blue light and stuck it to the roof using its magnet on the bottom. After that, they sped off chasing the spotlight.

When they got the truck stopped, they found men with loaded guns. They seized the firearms and the spotlight, then issued them all a citation for illegal night hunting from the road. After finishing the ticket writing, they decided to go back and hide their truck in the same spot.

Staying in the same area after catching a bunch was something I disliked. I always felt other poachers knew I was around after blue lights had come on. But on this night, Joe and Tom decided to try it. They were glad they did.

It wasn't long before a second vehicle came down the road, shining a spotlight. Once again, it was time to smack that old blue light onto the roof and get this second bunch. Similarly, the two officers caught some men with a spotlight and several loaded guns. A second round of citation writing took place.

After catching these two bunches of poachers from the same spot on the same night, the officers looked at each other and said, "Why not?"

So, back to the exact location, they went and hid. They got backed up in their field to hide one more time. Late into the night, yet another truck and spotlight came calling. The game warden's vehicle (already weighed down with seized guns) took off once more to chase a group of poachers.

For a third time, they caught another bunch. They did all the same things again. There was barely any sitting room between all the guns for the two officers as they made their way home.

I have thought of this story often as I sat out on lonely stakeouts in the middle of nowhere. It was hard not to be jealous. Without the airplane flying, I could never catch over one bunch of spotlighters on a single night.

I always knew wildlife thrived in my part of the state because of men like Officers Joe Pillow and Tom Caudill.

Odds and Ends

With this job come moments that make you go, huh? You will see strange things and experience both moments of inspiration and bewilderment. In this chapter, I want to toss out a few of the odds and ends that come from life as a game warden.

I once received a call from a person in Franklin, KY. In the city was a mobile home trailer park near the McDonald's restaurant. The caller advised that someone in that trailer park was possessing wildlife illegally. They claimed this person was keeping a live raccoon.

Others had live raccoons. If you possessed them legally and got a wildlife permit from the state, then there was no problem. The caller, however, advised that these people did none of that. So, I dressed in a uniform, got in my state truck, and headed to the mobile home lot. I pictured in my mind what this would be like. Those thoughts were nowhere close.

I was already drawing some attention while driving slowly through the trailer park. The residents sensed I wasn't there for a social call. They followed the game warden's truck with their eyes like animals at a Serengeti watering hole watching a lion. I wasn't feeling very lionish. I pictured myself more like a hyena looking for a remnant to grab and run.

When I finally located my trailer, I expected the usual wire cage with the nasty water bowl sitting outside. There was no sign of that. So, I climbed the narrow, rickety steps and knocked on the front door.

Usually, I would have preferred doing it differently. Cold calling and wanting to see something inside a home didn't typically work out well. Today, however, these folks rolled out the red shag carpet. I asked them if they had a raccoon. They said, "Yes, it's right over here. Would you like to see it?" This welcome seemed way too easy.

I looked over, expecting to find that wire cage finally. Instead, I was looking at a baby's playpen. They certainly did have a live raccoon in it. They also had a live baby in it.

Trying to maintain my poker face, I walked over to check on the two in confinement. I immediately felt this was not safe for the baby. Soon, I changed my mind and started feeling sorry for the raccoon.

While my hosts made small talk with me, I watched the masked bandit do his best to avoid a laughing baby who kept trying to grab him. The raccoon would snarl and snap after each attempt and then change corners. Each change gave him a few seconds of peace as the baby had to have time to crawl and reposition before its next snatch-and-grab effort. Why the baby was not dripping blood, I do not know.

I had to give them the bad news. We would have to swap out the trash panda with a yellow rubber duck and a citation. Bandit was coming with me, and I'm sure he felt relieved.

I knew of another "Bandit" in this town. Police officer Bob Huber had a pet raccoon by that name. That one was legally permitted. It was quite a bit larger than its trailer court cousin. Bob treated his pet way better than most. Still, his masked outlaw often left marks on the lawman.

One day, I stopped by the police station and saw Officer Huber wearing a bandage on his nose. That's a conversation starter.

It wasn't my first time seeing medical wrappings on Bob, but this one was more noticeable. Of course, I had to smile and ask the question. Like the other answers before it, the response started with, "I was playing with Bandit and ...".

Not long after that, I noticed a sizeable hand-drawn cartoon on the city bulletin board. Police Officer Wayne May was a gifted artist with a sense of humor. He had drawn a cartoon picture of a tombstone that read, "R. I. P. Bandit." Beside the grave marker stood a battered, bandaged police officer with a smoking gun. The resemblance of Officer Huber was perfect.

We all knew Bob would never kill Bandit, no matter how many abrasions his pet caused, but I do believe he learned to keep his nose away from the cage.

Even though I encountered many things that left me bewildered, I occasionally ran into something inspirational. I never thought I could write a story about a wildlife law violator who inspired me, but I even ran into that one day.

My phone rang as it so often did. I picked it up to hear a young man wanting to turn someone in for breaking the law. The violator he planned to hand over was himself.

This incident was not the first time someone had contacted me to report that they had broken the law. It happened several times throughout the years. But this young man was different.

All the previous ones telling on themselves were just quick thinkers trying to get ahead of something. By that, I mean they knew someone had seen them and believed the hammer was about to drop. So, they wanted to strike first, then twist their story and hope for leniency. My current caller did not wish to obtain leniency. It was not what he was seeking. That was different.

I drove out to meet the young man who had called me. I could tell he was of the Amish or Mennonite faith. No one had seen him breaking the law, at least no one on this earth. I could quickly tell I was looking at genuine remorse. He started telling me his story.

He had been out hunting when he saw a large hawk. For whatever unknown reason, he decided to shoot it. He hit his target, and it fell out of the tree dead.

The young man walked over and picked up the hawk. He almost cried when he said, "I picked up that majestic bird and the Lord smote my heart." I won't ever forget those words.

No one on earth had seen this young man break a wildlife law, but someone who did see it was talking to him. He was sincerely remorseful and wanted to pay for his crime.

Over the years, game wardens can become jaded. When you have seen the things we have, it can make you think the worst of people. But sometimes, occasionally, God paints you a sunrise or sends someone your way to breathe back a little hope inside you. Even though he had broken the law and killed a beautiful creature, this young man gave me a brighter outlook.

I did go ahead and write him a citation. I felt justice arrived from somewhere else, but at the same time, I truly felt he wanted to do what was legal now and pay his fine. I sensed there was a need inside him to do this. It was the only citation I ever wrote where I came away inspired by someone who violated one of our laws.

Made in the USA
Middletown, DE
14 November 2024

64196109R00108